ROMANS

Here We Stand...Here We Live

A Devotional Study Guide

Written and Compiled by

Dr. Garry Baldwin

© 2017 by Dr. Garry Baldwin

All rights reserved.

Scripture references: Holy Bible, Holman Christian Standard, Pew, Maroon (Holman Bible Pub) © 2012

The Bible consists of sixty-six different books, composed by many different writers in three different languages under different circumstances; writers of almost every social rank: statesmen and peasants, kings, herdsmen, fishermen, priests, tax-gatherers, tentmakers; educated and uneducated; Jews and Gentiles; most of them unknown to each other and writing at various periods during the space of about 1600 years. And yet, after all, it is only one book dealing with only one subject in its numberless aspects and relations: the subject of man's redemption. It is God's Revelation of Truth... basic truth.

One book in the Bible seems to summarize the whole. It is Paul's letter to the Romans. Romans is the sixth book written in the New Testament. Paul wrote the book from Corinth around 56 AD. It is an Old and New Testament Gospel... this is why some even call it <u>the Gospel According to Paul.</u> It teaches us how to be a Believer. I do not mean in trying to do all the right things, but in understanding God's love, mercy, grace, and peace, one can respond to what God is doing around you.

I don't want to assume that everyone knows this character in the Bible, but I don't want to bore you with too many details. Paul was born about the same time as Jesus. He was raised in Tarsus, a town of wealthy and educated people, and he himself was trained and educated by the best of teachers in Jewish Law. He began his career as one that persecuted Christians until he met Jesus (in a vision, spiritually) on the Damascus road, accepted the Gospel message, and was born again.

Paul's Hebrew name was Saul and his Roman name, Paul.

As a dedicated missionary of Jesus, he wrote at least thirteen of the New Testament books of the Bible. So here we are in the study of one his most important letters. It was written to the Church in Rome, but you will discover in this study, it was written to you and me also. 2017 marked the 500th anniversary of the period known as the Reformation where Martin Luther, inspired by a verse in Romans, began his personal journey to understand and apply God's Word. This is the purpose of this study. I want you to read through these thoughts and understand where you stand on issues in our society today and live forth your convictions to influence and inform others of God's truths.

I want to thank the staff and lay leaders of Brookwood Baptist Church, in Burlington, N.C., who, over 20 years ago in 1997, helped put the original format of this study guide together. Together, we learned to stand in the faith and live our lives by God's Grace in that faith journey. Together we began this project.

This guide is to help the reader to walk through the letter of Romans and apply it to their faith walk today in order to live out their faith daily as they ask the LORD for directions and help. Begin in silence as you seek the presence of your Heavenly Father and God. Continue in confession as He convicts and cleanses your heart. Then, listen for a fresh Word from our LORD who will speak to you at your personal point of need. In such a time as this in our world, one has to know where they stand on issues that demand an example of that lifestyle. My prayer is that this study will allow you to join with me in a new period of personal reformation saying as the Church:

"Here We Stand...Here We Live"

My Daily Quiet Time Significant Journey Journal

(How to use your devotional guide)

As you begin your Daily Quiet Time follow the guide located on the right side of the page. Use this space to journal your thoughts and prayers.

1. **Ready** yourself for a **Fresh Encounter** (Seek and recognize God's presence as you begin your time.) *"Be silent before the LORD and wait expectantly for Him."* Psalm 37:7 Do this in Prayer using this ACTS guide:

   a. Adoration: (Praise and Worship)

   "Enter His gates with thanksgiving and His courts with praise: give thanks to Him and praise His name." Psalm 100:4

   b. Confession: (Repentance and Forgiveness)

   "...forgive us our sins, as we ourselves also forgive everyone in debt to us." Luke 11:4

   c. Thanksgiving:

   "Hallelujah! Give thanks to the LORD, for He is good: His faithful love endures forever." Psalm 106:1

2. **Read** God's Word.

Read today's Scripture and hear a **Fresh Word** from God. *"All scripture is inspired by God (God-breathed) and is profitable for teaching, for rebuking, for correcting, and for training in righteousness."* II Timothy 3:16

Then... as you journal...Write down your thoughts in the space provided and

3. **Respond** with the ***"Mind of Christ."***

This is your hearts response to God's Word. This may include questions where fuller understanding is needed as well as <u>petitions</u> for personal needs, and <u>intercession</u> for others. (Write them down here)

"I assure you, anything you ask the Father in My name, He will give you." John 16:23

Then…Continue to write down your reflections…

4. **Reflect** and listen to God's voice. (God's response to your prayers.) What is God saying to you? How has He answered your prayers?

"Call on me and I will answer you and tell you great and unsearchable things you do not know." Jeremiah 33:3

Then…

5. **Rely** on Jesus to help you live out these truths. (My response to what God has told me to do.)

"Those who hear the Word of God and keep it are blessed." Luke 11:28

Ask the Lord, "<u>What do you want me to do today?</u>"

    a. God's to-do list for today.
(List things you feel you need to do.)
    b. Put on the full Armor of God:

"Stand firm then, with the <u>belt of truth</u> buckled around your waist, with the <u>breastplate of righteousness</u> in place, and with your feet fitted with the <u>readiness that comes from the gospel of peace</u>. In addition to all this take up the <u>shield of faith</u>, with which you can extinguish all the flaming arrows of the evil one. Take the <u>helmet of salvation</u> and the <u>sword of the Spirit</u> which is the Word of God." Ephesians 6:14-18

"And pray in the Spirit on all occasions with all kinds of prayers and requests." Pray continually.

Week One - Day One

Romans 1: 1-6

Take a Good Look in the Mirror

We begin our journey in Romans chapter one with an introduction. It was customary in the First Century correspondence to commence with the writer's name, to state the name of the recipient of the letter, and to bring greetings. Paul does this and much more as he presents a simple, yet complex, glimpse at his heart, mind, and personal attitudes. Paul, first of all, sees himself as a slave of Christ Jesus. He uses the term **doulos**, translated servant, which means "one who is dedicated to serve with no personal rights". He also wanted to make it clear to the reader *Who's* servant he was. Paul was passionate about truth, but not just any truth... God's Truth. What he found to be vital Truth. God had revealed Himself to Paul supernaturally, and now Paul had a specific purpose. Also, he states his purpose: "set apart for the gospel of God." He had a sharply defined sense of destiny and purpose. Paul had met the Gospel face-to-face on that Damascus road and he knew this vital truth that had set him free and given him purpose. He goes on to clearly define this purpose so that there would be no mistakes. He was ready to make his stand in writing.

Paul felt the same about his readers of this letter. He believed all who have been called by God and have committed their lives to Christ Jesus need to know their Master and their purpose...where they stood. As you reflect today and begin this journey into Romans, ask yourself: "Do I know my Master?" "Do I know my purpose for being on this earth?" God wants you to be clear! Take a good look in the mirror today. Do you know where you stand and where you live?

1-13-2020

My Quiet Time Significant Journey Journal

1. **Ready yourself** for a Fresh encounter with God. Pray and ask God to speak to you. (Psalm 37:7)

2. **Read** the Scripture of the Day and prepare to hear a **Fresh Word** from God. (II Timothy 3:16-17)

3. **Respond** with the *"Mind of Christ"* by writing down what God has said to you through the Scripture and the devotional thoughts. (Jeremiah 33:3)

"Ask me and I will tell you remarkable secrets you do not know about things to come"

-Help me Lord to come to you with patience and a willingness to learn everytime.

4. **Reflect** as you *"Experience God"* by listening to His Voice and writing down your prayers and thoughts. (John 16:23) "... you will ask the father directly and he will grant your request" Use my name

-Thank you God that we no longer need to go through anyone to get to you

5. **Rely** on Jesus to help you live out these truths. (Luke 11:28) Ask, *"Lord, what do you want me to do today?"* (God's to-do list.)

-I am praying that my words are pleasing to you and will be just what is needed/nothing more

(Pray for strength as you put on the Full Armor of God.)

Week One - Day Two

Romans 1: 7-12

Encouragement

Paul continues his greetings to all the churches at Rome with an affectionate "saintly" greeting and affirmation. His purpose is clear in writing this letter: to mutually encourage and be encouraged. He declares God's grace and God's peace. Grace gives us the ability to live the victorious Christian life, abundant and free from the power of sin. It is the righteousness of God freely given to us. God's peace is God's fullness. In the Old Testament, it means completeness, soundness and wholeness as a person. But in the New Testament, the Gospel in Christ is a message of peace from God to men. The peace that Christ brought is primarily spiritual peace from and with God. It is peace in the heart and only found in a personal relationship with the Lord Jesus Christ. (Romans 5:1) This is the message God gives us to share. We know it as born again children of God and must share it with others. As believers in the Lord Jesus Christ, it is clear that we can and must grow with, and through, each other. You do not have all the answers or all the gifts. The body of Christ is diverse and we really do need each other. "No man is an island, no man stands alone!" We all need to seek to get to know each other and encourage one another. People who are different from you can teach you a lot. Is there someone in your Church who can grow by your faith so you can grow by theirs? You see, as you give away your faith as a blessing to someone else, they grow spiritually. As a result, you grow as God Himself strengthens you. The opposite is true, as well: as you receive a blessing of faith from others in the body of Christ, you grow in the Lord. Let's get encouraged today as we encourage one another.

1-4-2020

My Quiet Time Significant Journey Journal

1.   Ready yourself for a Fresh encounter with God. Pray and ask God to speak to you. (Psalm 37:7)

2.   Read the Scripture of the Day and prepare to hear a **Fresh Word** from God. (II Timothy 3:16-17)

3.   Respond with the ***"Mind of Christ"*** by writing down what God has said to you through the Scripture and the devotional thoughts. (Jeremiah 33:3)

- I believe God is telling me, I still have much to learn, not just from him but from others.

4.   Reflect as you ***"Experience God"*** by listening to His Voice and writing down your prayers and thoughts. (John 16:23)

- I believe God is calling me to be an example even to my enemies.

5.   Rely on Jesus to help you live out these truths. (Luke 11:28) Ask, **"Lord, what do you want me to do today?"**   (God's to-do list.)

- Please guide me in my relationships and business dealings as well Lord (RFG*)

(Pray for strength as you put on the Full Armor of God.)

Week One - Day Three

Romans 1:13-17

Enthusiastic Commitment

People get tired, discouraged, bored, and disillusioned, with the result being that both they and their work suffer. At the time of writing to the Roman church, Paul had probably been actively engaged in his ministry for almost thirty hectic, energy-sapping years. He had endured enough hardship and been exposed to enough trauma and excitement to last most people for half a dozen lifetimes. He had been triumphant, through persistent problems, but he had an **Enthusiastic Commitment** to his purpose and task.

At almost sixty years of age, Paul presents the thought in these verses, in a mature way, yet with youthful vigor. Paul placed no limits on his ministry. He lived with a constant sense of obligation to Jesus. He felt obliged to minister to "whosoever" because that is the depth of the Gospel. Over 500 years ago, Martin Luther's life was changed by Romans 1:17. He says, "For in *it*," in the gospel, "the righteousness of God is revealed from faith to faith, as it is written, 'the just shall live by faith.'" This is a verse taken from the book of Habakkuk in the Old Testament that is cited three times in the New Testament. And so, the lights came on for Luther. And he began to understand that what Paul was speaking of here was a righteousness that God in His grace was making available to those who would receive it passively, not those who would achieve it actively, but that would receive it by faith, and by which a person could be reconciled to a holy and righteous God. Are you enthusiastically committed to the Gospel of Jesus Christ? Are you ready for your "reformation"? It is life! It is all that really matters!

1-15-2020

My Quiet Time Significant Journey Journal

1. Ready yourself for a Fresh encounter with God. Pray and ask God to speak to you. (Psalm 37:7)

2. Read the Scripture of the Day and prepare to hear a **Fresh Word** from God. (II Timothy 3:16-17)

3. Respond with the **"Mind of Christ"** by writing down what God has said to you through the Scripture and the devotional thoughts. (Jeremiah 33:3)

God has reminded me through scripture that I am called to serve those less fortunate. If I have been given gifts, I need to use them to serve others.

4. Reflect as you **"Experience God"** by listening to His Voice and writing down your prayers and thoughts. (John 16:23)

- I pray that I have the enthusiastic commitment Paul had even with our many years in our service.

5. Rely on Jesus to help you live out these truths. (Luke 11:28) Ask, **"Lord, what do you want me to do today?"** (God's to-do list.)

Please continue to show me when I am wrong in my judgements of others.

(Pray for strength as you put on the Full Armor of God.)

Week One - Day Four

Romans 1:18-20

"Without Excuse"

The righteousness of God is the theme of both the Gospel Paul preached and the Epistle he wrote to the Romans. In order to understand the righteousness of God, one must understand God's thinking and man's thinking. The fact that God is righteous – or is always "in the right" – is both a challenge and a comfort. The challenge comes to mankind through realizing that the rightness of human action must be determined, not by different moral standards of society, but by the unchanging revelation of an eternal God. The comfort comes by knowing that God is always "in the right" or righteous. Man must learn to turn to God for wisdom, guidance, and salvation. Thus, the closer a man gets to the rightness of God, the more he recognizes that unrighteousness of himself. (an Isaiah 6 mentality)

The Gospel, therefore, recognizes this, and in its revelation of the righteousness of God shows how mankind can have his situation changed. Romans shows this truth both spiritually and legally. We see that the wrath of God (defined as the natural consequences of sin) is not a problem to avoid but to understand. Divine wrath should not be confused with human wrath.

And God loved us so much He made Himself evident throughout creation. He did not want anyone to make the excuse that they "haven't heard". The heavens declare the Glory of God. Creation demonstrates and illustrates the "eternal power and divine nature" of God. Man is without excuse. Now, God calls us to point out those truths lovingly and specifically to ourselves, our families, our friends, and our world. Here we stand, Here we live! Let's share these truths.

1-16-2020

My Quiet Time Significant Journey Journal

1. **Ready yourself** for a Fresh encounter with God. Pray and ask God to speak to you. (Psalm 37:7)

2. **Read** the Scripture of the Day and prepare to hear a **Fresh Word** from God. (II Timothy 3:16-17)

3. **Respond** with the **"Mind of Christ"** by writing down what God has said to you through the Scripture and the devotional thoughts. (Jeremiah 33:3)

Through the devotional God is telling me to knock out my excuses, since he didn't make excuses to save us though we didn't deserve it

4. **Reflect** as you **"Experience God"** by listening to His Voice and writing down your prayers and thoughts. (John 16:23)

I need to turn to God for wisdom, guidance, salvation and help.

5. **Rely** on Jesus to help you live out these truths. (Luke 11:28) Ask, **"Lord, what do you want me to do today?"** (God's to-do list.)

I am praying that I turn to God first before my own judgement in my problems.

(Pray for strength as you put on the Full Armor of God.)

Week One - Day Five

Romans 1:20-22

Ignorance or Responsibility

Paul not only insisted that God has revealed himself to mankind (vs. 20), but he focused on the fact that man's refusal to glorify God as God is as unacceptable to God as suppressing the truth. To glorify God is to give outward praise as a natural response to the understanding of God's investment in our lives. In other words, to "praise God from Whom all blessings flow." The knowledge of God that even the most primitive man has available to him is enough to lead him to an attitude of glorification and thanksgiving to God. Ideally, mankind, in the normal course of the events of life, would be sensitive enough to make the transition from knowledge about God to response to God. But the reality of the situation, however absurd, is that man chooses not to respond adequately, and then accounts for his actions as not really understanding. The situation is similar to how children respond to parents: "What did I do?" The claim of ignorance rather than responsibility is just another indictment against us all. *"Professing to be wise, we become fools."*

May we all realize our responsibilities to God. We must stand up for God's truth and understand our assignment from God as we live out our "significant journeys" for His Glory. Someone is watching. Someone is waiting to hear from us. We must make that commitment to share.

1-17-2020

My Quiet Time Significant Journey Journal

1. Ready yourself for a Fresh encounter with God. Pray and ask God to speak to you. (Psalm 37:7)

2. Read the Scripture of the Day and prepare to hear a **Fresh Word** from God. (II Timothy 3:16-17)

3. Respond with the **"Mind of Christ"** by writing down what God has said to you through the Scripture and the devotional thoughts. (Jeremiah 33:3)

- We must stand up for God's truth and understand our assignment from God.

4. Reflect as you **"Experience God"** by listening to His Voice and writing down your prayers and thoughts. (John 16:23)

"Professing to be wise, we become fools."

5. Rely on Jesus to help you live out these truths. (Luke 11:28) Ask, **"Lord, what do you want me to do today?"** (God's to-do list.)

Lord, help me to catch myself when I become to confident in my own skills.

(Pray for strength as you put on the Full Armor of God.)

Week One - Day Six

Romans 1:23-28

Man's Substitution for Creation

God has shown Himself to man "since creation." It is true to say that man began to reject the obvious revelation of God from the earliest times. The similarity between the list of idols Paul gives here in Romans 1:23-28 is not accidental. Neither is the obvious link between Paul's use of the word "images" here and in Genesis 1:26.

Many have reversed the divine order by making God in man's own image and after his own likeness, and even worse. The root of the problem is in man's utterly arrogant preoccupation with himself. We focus so much on our own needs, our own wants, our own happiness, and our own satisfaction that we only seek God to fulfill all our desires. We are more concerned with pleasing ourselves than with knowing God's will and plan for our lives. So God allows man to teach himself a lesson. If man wants to be "god", then God will allow the natural consequences (wrath) of this sin to be the judge that teaches the lesson. If man makes such a substitution for satisfaction, then man's creation will show itself deficient. Look around our world today and see the "natural consequences of sin." God's wrath is evident.

God is simply, yet profoundly, making His point so *all* mankind will understand and be "without excuse." We must point out these truths lovingly and specifically. We cannot compromise His truths. Here we stand... Here we live!

1-20-2020

My Quiet Time Significant Journey Journal

1.   Ready yourself for a Fresh encounter with God. Pray and ask God to speak to you. (Psalm 37:7)

2.   Read the Scripture of the Day and prepare to hear a **Fresh Word** from God. (II Timothy 3:16-17)

3.   Respond with the *"Mind of Christ"* by writing down what God has said to you through the Scripture and the devotional thoughts. (Jeremiah 33:3)

God reminding us of what we are without him.

4.   Reflect as you *"Experience God"* by listening to His Voice and writing down your prayers and thoughts. (John 16:23)

God loves us enough to allow us to make our own decisions but is always waiting for us.

5.   Rely on Jesus to help you live out these truths. (Luke 11:28) Ask, **"Lord, what do you want me to do today?"**   (God's to-do list.)

I think God wants to remind me that he knows what he's talking about and will let me come to my own conclusions but has already provided me with what I need.

(Pray for strength as you put on the Full Armor of God.)

God gave them over to their sinful desires

Week One - Day Seven

Romans 1:28-32

Rational Lies

Without going into the details of the record of human misdemeanors listed here, we cannot avoid seeing that the problems of Paul's days and times were very similar to our own. It is easy to see it all happening before us. The shame of the situation is a "healthy shame" that should bring a sense of repentance and grief. A great reaching out for righteousness, restoration, and renewal ought to be the greatest of human longing, but it seems such is not the case. The appalling truth is that those who could reasonably be expected to react towards God in such a way do the opposite, as Paul states in verse 32. This leads us to consider one more negative attitude of man: rationalization. We make excuses and give reasons for sin. God says something is wrong. God says something is sin, and we rationalize with excuses and the public opinion of man.

We are living in the same society, because it is the society of mankind. These thoughts in Chapter One have led us to the sober understanding that we need God. If we simply focus on man trying to do right and be good, it will always lead to the rejection of God, for mankind will seek to do it "his way." It is only when we seek God and "His righteousness" (Matthew 6:33), that we can even begin to become righteous. (II Corinthians 5:21) Man cannot do it! We all need Jesus! Quit trying to rationalize and think you can live right on your own. Do not believe the lies of the world no matter how reasonable they seem. Rational lies are never truthful. To rationalize means to believe "rational lies".

1-21-2020

My Quiet Time Significant Journey Journal

1. Ready yourself for a Fresh encounter with God. Pray and ask God to speak to you. (Psalm 37:7)

2. Read the Scripture of the Day and prepare to hear a **Fresh Word** from God. (II Timothy 3:16-17)

3. Respond with the *"Mind of Christ"* by writing down what God has said to you through the Scripture and the devotional thoughts. (Jeremiah 33:3)

We make excuses and give reasons for sin

4. Reflect as you *"Experience God"* by listening to His Voice and writing down your prayers and thoughts. (John 16:23)

Sometimes we think we are more accepting & merciful than God.

5. Rely on Jesus to help you live out these truths. (Luke 11:28) Ask, *"Lord, what do you want me to do today?"* (God's to-do list.)

If we focus on man trying to do right + be good, it will always lead to the rejection of God.

(Pray for strength as you put on the Full Armor of God.)

Help me to realize I need to stand up for you first

Week Two - Day One

Romans 2:1-3

Any Excuse? Any Escape?

Sometimes we think too highly of ourselves. People tend to have a false moral opinion of themselves because their standard of righteousness is based on other people. We easily see the speck in our brother's eye but miss the beam in our own. This is because there is a distorted perspective. People may consider themselves heaven-bound because they are "good," moral, and ethical individuals. They may hate crime and cry out for swift and unmerciful justice. Yet, the lost many times may not realize that they are under the same condemnation. *"The judgment of God... is based on truth."* (v. 2) The truth is the Word of God which says, "All we like sheep have gone astray: we have turned every one to his own way." (Isaiah 53:6) Every man, woman, and child is born with a sin nature inherited from Adam. David speaks for all when he says, *"Indeed, I was guilty when I was born; I was sinful when my mother conceived me."* (Psalm 51:5) Thus, we all are guilty in God's sight when we commit that first sin. Our moral standard must be compared to God's holiness.

It is said that for someone to be saved, they must first acknowledge that they are lost. That is what Paul is doing here. He is telling Gentile pagans and Hebrew hypocrites alike that their good words and their ritualistic religions are empty and vain. Every man is without excuse (v. 1) and every man is without escape. (Romans 2:3) But Praise God, there is hope! Paul will later tell how God in His love has thrown us a lifeline, a bloodline that flows from Emmanuel's veins.

1-22-2020

My Quiet Time Significant Journey Journal

1. Ready yourself for a Fresh encounter with God. Pray and ask God to speak to you. (Psalm 37:7)

2. Read the Scripture of the Day and prepare to hear a **Fresh Word** from God. (II Timothy 3:16-17)

No excuse

3. Respond with the *"Mind of Christ"* by writing down what God has said to you through the Scripture and the devotional thoughts. (Jeremiah 33:3)

- Do you think you will escape Gods judgment?
- Judge + be judged

4. Reflect as you *"Experience God"* by listening to His Voice and writing down your prayers and thoughts. (John 16:23)

"All we sheep have gone astray"

We all fall short

5. Rely on Jesus to help you live out these truths. (Luke 11:28) Ask, *"Lord, what do you want me to do today?"* (God's to-do list.)

○ Our moral standard must be compared to Gods holiness

"Every man is without excuse

(Pray for strength as you put on the Full Armor of God.)

Help me please not to judge

Week Two - Day Two

Romans 2:4

Repent!

God desires for people to live holy, Spirit-filled lives in Christ Jesus. "Repentance" is a change of attitude or thinking about sin, and a turning from sin toward God. God is patient with us, not willing that any should perish, but wanting everyone to come to repentance. (II Peter 3:9b) God is tolerant of unbelievers (for a while) because He wants every person to have the opportunity to turn from sinful self to Jesus Christ as Lord of their lives. Perhaps, people will see how precious and loving God is by deferring His judgment. People respond more when they see the love of God rather than the fear of His wrath. (Revelation 9:20-21) *"We love because He first loved us."* (I John 4:19) God is just so that those who reject the truth will be speechless at the Great White Throne judgment.

We could never repent unless the Holy Spirit first brings conviction. Even repentance is an act of grace, which comes from God. (II Corinthians 7:10, II Timothy 2:25) Believer, is there any sin in your life? God is allowing you time to self-judge and confess it before He disciplines you. (I Corinthians 11:31-32; I John 1:9) God corrects His children so they may yield the fruit of righteousness and holiness. We are to be molded and shaped into the image of the Son of God. So God wants us to Repent! Do not show contempt for God's patience! Pray as David did in Psalm 139:23-24: *"Search me, O God and know my heart: test me, and know my concerns: See if there be any offensive way in me, and lead me in the everlasting way."*

1-23-2020

My Quiet Time Significant Journey Journal

1. Ready yourself for a Fresh encounter with God. Pray and ask God to speak to you. (Psalm 37:7)

2. Read the Scripture of the Day and prepare to hear a **Fresh Word** from God. (II Timothy 3:16-17)

3. Respond with the *"Mind of Christ"* by writing down what God has said to you through the Scripture and the devotional thoughts. (Jeremiah 33:3)

God allows you time to self judge and confess it before he disciplines you.

4. Reflect as you *"Experience God"* by listening to His Voice and writing down your prayers and thoughts. (John 16:23)

- God's kindness is intended to lead you to repentance

5. Rely on Jesus to help you live out these truths. (Luke 11:28) Ask, *"Lord, what do you want me to do today?"* (God's to-do list.)

We could never repent unless the Holy Spirit first brings conviction.

(Pray for strength as you put on the Full Armor of God.)

"Search me O God!"

Week Two - Day Three

Romans 2:5-11

Judgment Day or Days?

God's judgment is fair. People will get what they have earned with favoritism. (Romans 2:6, 11) Because of the hardness of the unrepentant heart, the lost person <u>is storing up</u> God's wrath as deposits in a reservoir. When the dam breaks on the day of God's judgment, God's anger will pour on wicked souls in unmerciful punishment. Romans 2:7-10 does <u>not</u> imply that salvation is by works. Salvation is a gift (grace) from God, received by faith when a person believes in Jesus Christ and His finished work and trusts, surrenders, and commits his life to the Lordship of Christ. (Ephesians 2:8-9) Yet, even now, God's judgment is based on works (as it is on truth). (Romans 2:2) We are <u>acquitted</u> because Jesus submitted Himself for us, bore our punishment, and paid our sin debt in full! How could we not love and obey Him? But, the wrath of God is still seen by those who are disobedient. A heart that is regenerated will habitually do good works. This is the evidence (not cause) of being "born again." Conversely, a rotten tree yields rotten fruit.

God desires to give all people glory, honor, immortality, eternal life and peace. The choice to accept or reject this gift is ours. God's gift is <u>His Son.</u> *"For the grace of God has appeared, with salvation for all people, instructing us to deny godlessness and worldly lusts and to live in a sensible, righteous, and godly way in the present age, while we wait for the blessed hope and the appearing of the glory of our great God and Savior, Jesus Christ. He gave Himself for us to redeem us from all lawlessness and to cleanse for Himself a special people, eager to do good works. (Titus 2:11-14)*

1-24-2020

My Quiet Time Significant Journey Journal

1. Ready yourself for a Fresh encounter with God. Pray and ask God to speak to you. (Psalm 37:7)

the lost person is storing up wrath

2. Read the Scripture of the Day and prepare to hear a **Fresh Word** from God. (II Timothy 3:16-17)

3. Respond with the **"Mind of Christ"** by writing down what God has said to you through the Scripture and the devotional thoughts. (Jeremiah 33:3)

- God repays each person according to what they have done.

4. Reflect as you **"Experience God"** by listening to His Voice and writing down your prayers and thoughts. (John 16:23)

11. God does not show favoritism
His judgement is fair

5. Rely on Jesus to help you live out these truths. (Luke 11:28) Ask, **"Lord, what do you want me to do today?"** (God's to-do list.)

- A heart that is regenerated will habitually do good works.

(Pray for strength as you put on the Full Armor of God.)

I will live for you from here on out!

Week Two – Day Four

Romans 2:12-16

Do You Have a "Life" Sentence?

If we have trusted Jesus Christ as our Lord and Savior, we have been pronounced "not guilty" (justified). We even have Christ's righteousness imputed (put in us by His Spirit). Notice the closeness in the Greek of these two words: "to justify" = dikaioo; and "righteous" = dikaios. Sinless Jesus became sin under God's judgment so that we might be made in Him, God's righteousness. (2 Corinthians 5:21) The person who does not have Christ in their heart stands condemned. (John 3:18, 36) Those who know God's Word and reject Christ will receive the greater punishment. With greater revelation of truth comes greater responsibility. A man could be justified by the Law if he kept every point of it. But, that's the problem. No one can do it! If we fail in one point of the Law, we are guilty of violating all of the Law. (James 2:10-12, Galatians 3:10, Deuteronomy 27:26) Even the Gentiles (those without the Law) are without excuse. God has given every person a conscience, which is a moral barometer of what is right and wrong. Yet, they are all guilty because they have violated their conscience and rejected creation's illustration. As a result of sin, our consciences have been perverted; it may be weak, defiled or seared. Everyone needs their consciences cleansed by the blood of Jesus. (Hebrews 9:14) God is the Justifier and the Judge. Man will be judged according to the truth by the Son of God. Even believers will stand before the Judgment Seat of Christ (not for salvation, but for the reward, or loss thereof, of their works). Every secret will be revealed. Every thought published. Motives for our service will be tested by fire. This is a sobering expectation. (II Corinthians 5:10, Ecclesiastes 12:14, Luke 8:17)

1-27-2020

My Quiet Time Significant Journey Journal

1.   Ready yourself for a Fresh encounter with God. Pray and ask God to speak to you. (Psalm 37:7)

2.   Read the Scripture of the Day and prepare to hear a **Fresh Word** from God. (II Timothy 3:16-17)

3.   Respond with the *"Mind of Christ"* by writing down what God has said to you through the Scripture and the devotional thoughts. (Jeremiah 33:3)

- Jesus became sin under God

4.   Reflect as you *"Experience God"* by listening to His Voice and writing down your prayers and thoughts. (John 16:23)

- Those who know God and reject him will have a more severe punishment.

5.   Rely on Jesus to help you live out these truths. (Luke 11:28) Ask, **"Lord, what do you want me to do today?"**   (God's to-do list.)

God gave each of us a concious

(Pray for strength as you put on the Full Armor of God.)

o Not just hearing but doing
o Every secret revealed.

Week Two – Day Five

Romans 2:17-24

Walk the Talk

What we say we believe needs to be clearly evident in how we live. Jesus condemned the hypocrisy of the Pharisees regarding the Law. In 17 verses of Matthew 23:13-29, He called them "hypocrites" eight times and "blind" five times. They fancied themselves as guides, light, and teachers of the Law (Romans 2:19-20), yet they did not observe it. When God gave the Law to Israel, He expected to receive glory when the heathen nations noticed God's presence with Israel as they obeyed the Law. (Deuteronomy 4:6-8) But sin dishonors God, profanes His Name, and ruins the witness of His people.

Christian, is your life pleasing to God? Does it lead people to Jesus or does it turn them off? Is where you stand how you live? The world hates religious phonies. Do you steal from your employer (measurable and immeasurable things)? Do you rob God of His tithe? Do you tell "white" lies? Do you laugh at corrupt jokes? Do you commit adultery in action or lustful thought? Is your pride a stench to God and unbelievers alike? Does your worry, fear, or anxiety reveal to others that you do not think that God can handle your problem? Does your life exhibit, exude, and exemplify the love, grace, holiness, and power of Jesus Christ to transform a life? Or do you give the word "Christian" a bad name? Do the enemies of God have fuel to blaspheme God because of you? This is what Nathan told David regarding the fruit of his sin with Bathsheba. (II Samuel 12:14) In verse 24, Paul quotes Isaiah 52:5 and Ezekiel 36:21-22. These passages continue in their texts to say that God will avenge His name because His name is holy!

1-28-2020

My Quiet Time Significant Journey Journal

1.   Ready yourself for a Fresh encounter with God. Pray and ask God to speak to you. (Psalm 37:7)

2.   Read the Scripture of the Day and prepare to hear a **Fresh Word** from God. (II Timothy 3:16-17)

3.   Respond with the *"Mind of Christ"* by writing down what God has said to you through the Scripture and the devotional thoughts. (Jeremiah 33:3)

Do you practice what you preach?

Do you give the name "Christian" a bad rap?

4.   Reflect as you *"Experience God"* by listening to His Voice and writing down your prayers and thoughts. (John 16:23)

- God condemns hypocrasy
- Sin ruins your witness to people

5.   Rely on Jesus to help you live out these truths. (Luke 11:28) Ask, ***"Lord, what do you want me to do today?"***   (God's to-do list.)

Is where you stand how you live?

(Pray for strength as you put on the Full Armor of God.)

- I pray my life leads people to Jesus

Week Two – Day Six

Romans 2:25-27

Holy Lives Wholly To God

Circumcision was important to the Jew. It was man's response to the covenant that God made with Abraham. God commanded that Abraham, the males of his household, and his descendants be circumcised in obedience. (Genesis 17:10-14) Yet, if the Law (or Mosaic Covenant) were broken, what is the value of circumcision? It would be a token ritual of no worth. Paul says that disobedience to the Law makes the Jew as a Gentile heathen. Obedience to God comes from love that is in the heart. Jesus said, *"These people honor Me with their lips; but their heart is far from Me."* (Matthew 15:8) Christian, we are told by Jesus to be "salt." Salt was a flavoring agent used as a preservative against spoilage. Our witness and lives must be holy, sanctified, and an honor to Jesus Christ. We will either influence the world or the world will influence us. Beware! If we lose our testimony by a sinful or compromised life, we are useless to do Kingdom work. Only through the cleansing power of Christ can one be restored to usefulness. Saltless salt is worthless to the souls that need it. Jesus said, *"It is therefore good for nothing, but to be cast out, and to be trodden under foot of men."* (Matthew 5:13) *"It is neither fit for the land, nor yet for the dunghill; but men cast it out."* (Luke 14:35)

May others see (and hear) Jesus in us! May our lives be Holy, Wholly to God!

1-29-2020

My Quiet Time Significant Journey Journal

1. Ready yourself for a Fresh encounter with God. Pray and ask God to speak to you. (Psalm 37:7)

2. Read the Scripture of the Day and prepare to hear a **Fresh Word** from God. (II Timothy 3:16-17)

3. Respond with the **"Mind of Christ"** by writing down what God has said to you through the Scripture and the devotional thoughts. (Jeremiah 33:3)

Circumsized vs uncircumsized, both on the same level.

4. Reflect as you **"Experience God"** by listening to His Voice and writing down your prayers and thoughts. (John 16:23)

Obedience to God comes from love that is in the heart.

"We are called to be Salt"

5. Rely on Jesus to help you live out these truths. (Luke 11:28) Ask, **"Lord, what do you want me to do today?"** (God's to-do list.)

"We will influence the world or it will influence us."

(Pray for strength as you put on the Full Armor of God.)

Week Two – Day Seven

Romans 2: 28-29

Righteous – Not a Rite

The rite (Holy act) of circumcision was the symbol of God's covenant with man through Abraham. It distinctly marked Abraham's descendants as the pure, set-apart possession of God. Yet, God wanted His people marked inwardly by the Holy Spirit rather than outwardly by a ritual to be heartlessly observed. Man looks on the outward appearance, but God looks upon the heart. (I Samuel 16:7) God desires a pure, clean, broken, and contrite heart of flesh, not a hardened stone.

Thus, Paul says that a person is not a Jew unless there is a change – a circumcision – of the heart. The same is true for Christians. We have to "ask Jesus to come into our hearts." Notice the effect of the circumcision of heart described by Paul in Galatians 3:26, 29 *"For you are all the children of God by faith in Christ Jesus… And if you be Christ's, then are you not* Abraham's seed, *and heirs according to the promise."*

To "circumcise" literally means, "to cut around." Allow the Holy Spirit to use the Sword of the Spirit, which is the Word of God, to cut around your heart. The Word is alive and powerful and sharper than any two-edged sword.

1-30-2020

My Quiet Time Significant Journey Journal

1. Ready yourself for a Fresh encounter with God. Pray and ask God to speak to you. (Psalm 37:7)

2. Read the Scripture of the Day and prepare to hear a **Fresh Word** from God. (II Timothy 3:16-17)

3. Respond with the *"Mind of Christ"* by writing down what God has said to you through the Scripture and the devotional thoughts. (Jeremiah 33:3)

29. "Praise is not from people but God

- God wanted his people marked inwardly by the Holy Spirit rather than outwardly by ritual.

4. Reflect as you *"Experience God"* by listening to His Voice and writing down your prayers and thoughts. (John 16:23)

"God desires a pure, clean, broken, + contrite heart of flesh, not a hardened stone."

- Circumsicion of the heart

5. Rely on Jesus to help you live out these truths. (Luke 11:28) Ask, *"Lord, what do you want me to do today?"* (God's to-do list.)

The word is sharper than any 2 edged sword

(Pray for strength as you put on the Full Armor of God.)

Week Three - Day One

Romans 3:1-8

God is Truth

Throughout these first three chapters Paul masterfully brings the whole world into court and shows that we all deserve judgment and condemnation because all have sinned. God has given us Creation, our Conscious, and Christ to reveal Himself and His truth to us. God is Truth explained and illustrated clearly to us all. We all are guilty and we all need God's love, forgiveness, mercy, and grace.

People can come up with many human arguments that God is unfair. But, the bottom line is that God is God and His ways are Truth. "Let God be true, and every man a liar." (Romans 3:4) God is Truth. Jesus said, "I am the way, the truth, and the life, no man comes to the Father but by Me." (John 14:6)

God began from creation giving His people inside evidence and profound truth of this love and grace. The advantage of the Jew is our advantage as well. We have been entrusted with the very Words of God. Therefore, like the Jew, is not our guilt even more self-evident? We have been shown the Truth of God and have still gone our own way. Now we must believe and receive it. We must stand strong in it and live it out in such a way that the entire world will see and respond. It is our responsibility now to go and tell this truth.

1-31-2020

My Quiet Time Significant Journey Journal

1. **Ready yourself** for a Fresh encounter with God. Pray and ask God to speak to you. (Psalm 37:7)

2. **Read** the Scripture of the Day and prepare to hear a **Fresh Word** from God. (II Timothy 3:16-17)

3. **Respond** with the *"Mind of Christ"* by writing down what God has said to you through the Scripture and the devotional thoughts. (Jeremiah 33:3)

   Our unrighteousness brings out Gods righteousness

4. **Reflect** as you *"Experience God"* by listening to His Voice and writing down your prayers and thoughts. (John 16:23)

   We all need Gods love + forgiveness

5. **Rely** on Jesus to help you live out these truths. (Luke 11:28) Ask, *"Lord, what do you want me to do today?"* (God's to-do list.)

   Our responsibility is to go tell his truth.

(Pray for strength as you put on the Full Armor of God.)

Week Three - Day Two

Romans 3:9-20

No One is Righteous

Some will say, "I'm not that bad," or "I just sin a little," or "Ninety percent of the time I'm a pretty good person." Here is an illustration that might help us in this: Suppose you were really thirsty. I mean really thirsty! And you took a gulp of your favorite beverage. Then I took a fly and put it into your glass and said, "Have another drink." Most would say, "I'd rather not." But, the fly was only a small thing; ninety percent of the drink was still good. Get the point? To a Holy God, our sin is kind of like that fly would be to us, but, oh, so much worse. You see, when we don't give God His rightful place in our lives, we are leading others toward Hell. When we don't stand for what we believe and live out His truths we are perverting God's absolute truth.

Sin means to miss the mark. The fact is that we have *all* missed the mark. But it is not that we have accidentally missed the mark. We have all purposely missed the mark. We have said, "I don't like this mark, I like this one," or "I don't really care what God says, I'm going to go this way." The evidence is pretty conclusive. We are all guilty before God. That's kind of depressing news.

But hold on to your seats, the Good News is yet to come!

2-3-2020

No one is righteous

My Quiet Time Significant Journey Journal

1. Ready yourself for a Fresh encounter with God. Pray and ask God to speak to you. (Psalm 37:7)

2. Read the Scripture of the Day and prepare to hear a **Fresh Word** from God. (II Timothy 3:16-17)

Rom. 3:9-20

3. Respond with the *"Mind of Christ"* by writing down what God has said to you through the Scripture and the devotional thoughts. (Jeremiah 33:3)

- Jews have no advantage
- "There is no one righteous, not even one"
- Through the law we become concious of our sin.

4. Reflect as you *"Experience God"* by listening to His Voice and writing down your prayers and thoughts. (John 16:23)

When we don't give God the rightfull place in our life we are leading them to Hell.

5. Rely on Jesus to help you live out these truths. (Luke 11:28) Ask, *"Lord, what do you want me to do today?"* (God's to-do list.)

We have all missed the mark

(Pray for strength as you put on the Full Armor of God.)

Don't want to pervert Gods absolute truth

Week Three - Day Three

Romans 3:21-26

We're Not Good Enough, But Jesus Is!

But now God has shown us a different way to be right with Him, and to be able to go to Heaven. It is not by being "good enough" and trying to keep His laws, but by a new way (though not new really, for the Old Testament told about it long ago - "to which the law and the Prophets testify" Romans 3:21.) Now God says He will accept us and make us right with Him and bring us to Heaven if we trust Jesus Christ to take away our sins. And we all can be saved in this way, by coming to Christ, no matter who we are or what we have been like.

If we evaluated humanity in baseball language we could sum it up this way: there are all kinds of ball players in the major leagues. There is the poor player who has a .180 batting average, the good player who hits .275, and then there is the batting champ who comes up with an amazing .374. But who bats 1.000? No one. No one bats 1.000. That is perfect!

God looks at man and sees him stepping up to the plate, grounding out, and striking out time and again, although once in a while he manages to get a double off the boards. For the best of us, it's a pretty poor performance. No one bats 1.000.

Therefore the Good News is not only for the "bad guys" who don't measure up, it's for the "good guys" who think they measure up, and it's for the "religious" who are trying to measure up. It is for us all. We are not good enough, but Jesus is.

2-4-2020

My Quiet Time Significant Journey Journal

1. Ready yourself for a Fresh encounter with God. Pray and ask God to speak to you. (Psalm 37:7)

Rom. 3:21-26 — Not Good enough but he is

2. Read the Scripture of the Day and prepare to hear a **Fresh Word** from God. (II Timothy 3:16-17)

3. Respond with the *"Mind of Christ"* by writing down what God has said to you through the Scripture and the devotional thoughts. (Jeremiah 33:3)

- Righteousness given through faith
- Redemption from Christ Jesus

4. Reflect as you *"Experience God"* by listening to His Voice and writing down your prayers and thoughts. (John 16:23)

"No one is perfect"

"We are not good enough but jesus is"

5. Rely on Jesus to help you live out these truths. (Luke 11:28) Ask, *"Lord, what do you want me to do today?"* (God's to-do list.)

(Pray for strength as you put on the Full Armor of God.)

Week Three - Day Four

Romans 3:23-31

Justified by God

Jesus paid it all! All to Him I owe!

God has provided for our salvation. He came into the world in the person of Jesus Christ and suffered for us on a bloody and terrible cross. God allowed His only Son to take our sin upon Himself so that we could be "justified". Justified?

To be "justified" before God means that God's justice has been satisfied through the substitutionary death of His Son, Jesus Christ. Christ paid the penalty for our sin, and He also removed the guilt for our sin. This last point, on guilt, is an important fact that many Christians overlook, or never really understands. Pretend that you were drunk driving and you killed someone. What a horrible thought! Imagine being brought before the judge. Picture him slamming down his gavel and saying "Guilty! Take this person away." As they are leading you away he says, "Wait, I want to take your place." The guards let you go and take the judge to the electric chair. He dies in your place, and you are set free. That is just an illustration, but isn't that what Jesus did for us?

The word justified can also be translated "declared righteous." Because of Christ, and through faith in Him, we are declared "not guilty, but righteous." Just as if we had never sinned.

2-5-2020

My Quiet Time Significant Journey Journal

1. Ready yourself for a Fresh encounter with God. Pray and ask God to speak to you. (Psalm 37:7)

Rom 3:23-31 (Jesus paid it all)

2. Read the Scripture of the Day and prepare to hear a **Fresh Word** from God. (II Timothy 3:16-17)

3. Respond with the **"Mind of Christ"** by writing down what God has said to you through the Scripture and the devotional thoughts. (Jeremiah 33:3)

To be justified before God means justice has been met through Christ Sacrifice

4. Reflect as you **"Experience God"** by listening to His Voice and writing down your prayers and thoughts. (John 16:23)

"Judge taking place for Criminal Analogy"

5. Rely on Jesus to help you live out these truths. (Luke 11:28) Ask, **"Lord, what do you want me to do today?"** (God's to-do list.)

Justified = declared righteouss

(Pray for strength as you put on the Full Armor of God.)

Week Three - Day Five

Romans 3:23-26

Grace

It has been said that we need to learn most things six times before we really learn it, and can apply it to our lives. So let's look at this passage again. But wait! I encourage you to read and meditate on the Scripture passage first, and ask God what He wants to say to you before you read this commentary. Write down what you sense God is wanting to teach you, then read this side and journal any further thoughts. "Being justified by His <u>grace</u> through the redemption that is in Christ Jesus. . ." (Romans 3:24). Grace means unmerited favor, undeserved love, or an undeserved gift.

There is only one word for God's grace - ***amazing***.

He paid a debt He did not owe, I owed a debt I could not pay

I needed someone to wash my sins away

and now I sing a brand new song, **Amazing Grace** all day long

Christ Jesus paid the debt that I could never pay!

(1977 Ellis J. Crum, Publisher Used by Permission CCLI License # 2615844)

One can only try to illustrate grace... Grace is like getting two more days to complete an assignment even though you've goofed off for six weeks and missed the deadline. Grace is getting another chance, even though you haven't earned it or deserved it. (You may not even want it!) But no earthly analogy really explains God's Grace. God's unmerited love and mercy are available to all people, even those who hate Him. When a person is truly sorry about his sin, and when he trusts Christ to be his personal Savior from sin, God freely forgives and accepts him, no matter what he has done. Only God could offer Grace like that!
Amazing!

2-6-2020

My Quiet Time Significant Journey Journal

1. Ready yourself for a Fresh encounter with God. Pray and ask God to speak to you. (Psalm 37:7)

Rom 3:23-20 "Grace"

2. Read the Scripture of the Day and prepare to hear a **Fresh Word** from God. (II Timothy 3:16-17)

3. Respond with the *"Mind of Christ"* by writing down what God has said to you through the Scripture and the devotional thoughts. (Jeremiah 33:3)

- For all have sinned + fall short of the glory of God
- Grace = unmerited favor, undeserved love/gift

4. Reflect as you *"Experience God"* by listening to His Voice and writing down your prayers and thoughts. (John 16:23)

- God's Grace is amazing

5. Rely on Jesus to help you live out these truths. (Luke 11:28) Ask, *"Lord, what do you want me to do today?"* (God's to-do list.)

Only God could offer the grace that freely forgives + accepts

(Pray for strength as you put on the Full Armor of God.)

You payed a debt you didn't owe

Week Three - Day Six

Romans 3:23-27

Redemption

We are justified freely by God's grace (unmerited love), through the redemption that is in Christ Jesus. Redemption involves payment. Redemption means "releasing from bondage by payment of a price." The idea of ransom is involved. Years ago, Frank Sinatra paid $240,000 for the return of Frank, Jr.

But Christ did more than pay a sum of money for our lives; He gave His own life as a ransom to deliver us from the bondage of sin. (Mark 10:45)

A story is told of a little boy who worked hard to build a nice toy sailboat. One day while sailing his little boat, the wind was strong and the little boat got away from him. He couldn't find it anywhere. Then one day he passed the toy store and there it was! His boat! He knew it was his because of some of the markings. He ran inside excitedly and told the clerk, "That's my boat! That's my boat!" The clerk said, "Son, I bought this boat. If you want it, you'll have to buy it." So the little boy ran home and worked hard until he could buy the boat. After several days he had enough, and he ran back and bought the boat. The clerk gave him the boat and the little boy hugged it tight as he went out the door. Then the little fellow said, "I made you and I bought you back; you're twice mine."

The Lord Jesus made us and He bought us back. We're twice His!

2-7-2020

My Quiet Time Significant Journey Journal

1. Ready yourself for a Fresh encounter with God. Pray and ask God to speak to you. (Psalm 37:7)

Rom 3:23-27 (Redemption)

2. Read the Scripture of the Day and prepare to hear a **Fresh Word** from God. (II Timothy 3:16-17)

3. Respond with the *"Mind of Christ"* by writing down what God has said to you through the Scripture and the devotional thoughts. (Jeremiah 33:3)

- Frank Sinatra analogy
- Christ gave his life for us (Mark 10:45)

4. Reflect as you *"Experience God"* by listening to His Voice and writing down your prayers and thoughts. (John 16:23)

"you are twice man analogy" (boy boat)

5. Rely on Jesus to help you live out these truths. (Luke 11:28) Ask, **"Lord, what do you want me to do today?"** (God's to-do list.)

We are twice his!

(Pray for strength as you put on the Full Armor of God.)

Week Three - Day Seven

Romans 3:25-31

Fully Pardoned by Faith

<u>Sacrifice of atonement</u> - The Greek for this phrase speaks of a sacrifice that satisfies the righteous wrath of God. Without this satisfaction all people are justly destined for eternal punishment. Man is separated from God - lost. He is a sinner. He is a captive in the hands of the Devil. Jesus came and died to pay the maximum price to buy us back, for we are rightfully His. The price was *His own life*, given on the cross. He purchased us not with silver or gold, but with His own blood. (See Acts 20:28.)

So what is there left for us to do?   Nothing.

Nothing except to receive God's Good News, believe it, and have faith. "Because our salvation is not based on our good deeds; it is based on what Christ has done and our faith in Him." (Romans 3:27) Faith in Christ changes us and makes us new persons. Faith, as Martin Luther put it, "...is a living, daring confidence in God's grace, so sure and certain that a man would stake his life on it a thousand times."

There is no magic in faith. Faith is simply our response to the salvation Christ obtained for us. We now face God unafraid. The penalty and guilt of sin is gone, paid for by God Himself. Religious rites and works do not make us right with God... and God doesn't expect them after we come to Christ either. We are *fully pardoned.* Our guilt is gone. We are not "on parole," earning our freedom or continuing to pay the debts for our crimes.

Wait a minute! You say, "Does that mean I can live any way I want to and not be concerned about obeying God's laws?" No way! Being pardoned by God makes you a new person. If you have truly accepted Christ, then you want to do His will. Your salvation is based on what Christ has done for you, and your faith in Christ as your Lord and Savior.

2-10-2020

My Quiet Time Significant Journey Journal

1. Ready yourself for a Fresh encounter with God. Pray and ask God to speak to you. (Psalm 37:7)

Rom 3:25-31 "Fully Pardoned by faith"

2. Read the Scripture of the Day and prepare to hear a **Fresh Word** from God. (II Timothy 3:16-17)

Sacrifice of atonement

3. Respond with the *"Mind of Christ"* by writing down what God has said to you through the Scripture and the devotional thoughts. (Jeremiah 33:3)

- Jesus paid the price to buy us back, "with his blood" (Acts 20:28)

- All we do is receive the Good news, believe it and have faith.

4. Reflect as you *"Experience God"* by listening to His Voice and writing down your prayers and thoughts. (John 16:23)

We are fully pardoned, not on parole.

- If you truly accepted Christ, you want to do his will.

5. Rely on Jesus to help you live out these truths. (Luke 11:28) Ask, *"Lord, what do you want me to do today?"* (God's to-do list.)

Our salvation is not based on our good deeds.
Rom 3:27

(Pray for strength as you put on the Full Armor of God.)

Week Four – Day One

Romans 4:1-3

"It's Not By Works"

As Paul continued his discussion on justification through faith in Christ, he used Abraham, a very familiar person in the Jewish faith to illustrate his point. Paul explained that Abraham, the father of faith and of the Jewish nation, was not justified by works, but by faith in God. Paul said, "If Abraham was justified by his works, then he has something to boast about." He went on to say, "but not before God."

If we are not careful,

we can become self-righteous in our thoughts.

It is easy to focus on ourselves and to pat ourselves on the back regarding how often we pray, read our Bibles, serve in the church, etc. If we are not careful, we can become self-righteous in our thoughts.

We must remember that Ephesians 2:8-9 says, "For you are saved by grace through faith and this is not of yourselves, it is God's gift, not from works, so that no one can boast."

Faith in the redemptive work of Christ is our only means of justification before God. Our righteousness apart from Christ is like filthy rags in the sight of God. (Isaiah 64:6)

2-11-2020

My Quiet Time Significant Journey Journal

1. Ready yourself for a Fresh encounter with God. Pray and ask God to speak to you. (Psalm 37:7)

Rom 4:3-1 "Its not by works"

2. Read the Scripture of the Day and prepare to hear a **Fresh Word** from God. (II Timothy 3:16-17)

Abraham believed God and it was credited to him as righteousness

3. Respond with the *"Mind of Christ"* by writing down what God has said to you through the Scripture and the devotional thoughts. (Jeremiah 33:3)

"If we are not careful, we can become self righteous in our thoughts"

4. Reflect as you *"Experience God"* by listening to His Voice and writing down your prayers and thoughts. (John 16:23)

"For you are saved by grace through faith"
Eph. 2:8-9

5. Rely on Jesus to help you live out these truths. (Luke 11:28) Ask, *"Lord, what do you want me to do today?"* (God's to-do list.)

Isaiah 64:6
We are not righteous apart from Christ.

(Pray for strength as you put on the Full Armor of God.)

Week Four – Day Two

Romans 4:5-8

"The Gift of Forgiveness"

There are many religions, ideas, and philosophies in the world that lead one to believe we must work our way into a right standing with God. They teach that if we do enough "good stuff," God will forgive us and let us into the Kingdom. The problem with that teaching is that God is perfect, and mankind is not. Romans 3:23 says "For all have sinned and fall short of the glory of God." We could *NEVER* do enough to meet God's standard of holiness. *None of us are perfect.*

But thank God for His wonderful grace. There are some words to a song that say, "He (Jesus) paid a debt He did not owe. I owed a debt I could not pay…" Jesus paid our sin debt, *HALLELUJAH!* Because of that, we can experience complete forgiveness through Christ. Think about this promise of forgiveness. "If we confess our sins, He is faithful and righteous to forgive us our sins and cleanse us from all unrighteousness." (I John 1:9)

Never run from God.

Forgiveness is simply a gift that cannot be earned. Remember that when you sin, you should *never run from God.* Run *to* Him, confess your sin (agree with God that you're wrong), and repent. God promises to cleanse you from all unrighteousness. Read Psalm 103:8-13.

Forgiveness is truly a blessing. It is a gift from God.

2-12-2020

My Quiet Time Significant Journey Journal

1. Ready yourself for a Fresh encounter with God. Pray and ask God to speak to you. (Psalm 37:7)

Rom 4:5-8 "The Gift of forgiveness"

2. Read the Scripture of the Day and prepare to hear a **Fresh Word** from God. (II Timothy 3:16-17)

3. Respond with the *"Mind of Christ"* by writing down what God has said to you through the Scripture and the devotional thoughts. (Jeremiah 33:3)

- God is perfect, mankind is not
- None of us are perfect.
- Jesus paid the debt we did not owe

4. Reflect as you *"Experience God"* by listening to His Voice and writing down your prayers and thoughts. (John 16:23)

- If we confess our sins he is faithful to forgive us. (1 John 1:9)

(Never Run from God, Run to him)

- We can't run anyway.

5. Rely on Jesus to help you live out these truths. (Luke 11:28) Ask, **"Lord, what do you want me to do today?"** (God's to-do list.)

of forgiveness is a gift that can be earned

☆ Agree with God you are wrong and repent

(Pray for strength as you put on the Full Armor of God.)

Week Four – Day Three

Romans 4:9-12

"In Christ Alone"

"In this blessedness only for the circumcised or also for the uncircumcised?" What did Paul ask? Basically, he asked if the idea of justification and forgiveness of sins was only for the Jews. Could it be for the Gentiles, too? Paul showed again, as we saw in Day One, that only faith in Jesus Christ gives us right standing with God. It does not matter if you are Jew or Greek, white or black, or this denomination or that.

Only faith in Jesus Christ gives us right standing with God.

God is looking for people to put their faith in Him. Then He can declare them righteous and give them the right to become children of God. (John 1:12) The focus that Paul is taking had to do with rituals and laws. The Christians that were raised in Jewish homes understood the importance of their religion and customs, but Paul is trying to help them understand that all of that was to point them to their need for God. It is not in doing everything "religiously right" to be righteousness, but to trust and believe in the LORD to be declared righteous. It does not hurt to "practice" your faith with religion and rituals that remind you of the greatness of your God and your faith. I mean we all love to go to Church, sing the hymns, take the Lord's Supper, etc. etc. But all these are useless "circumcisions" if not as a result of being made righteous by being born again by God's Spirit. Truly it is all "in Christ alone" that we put our trust for salvation.

2-13-2020

My Quiet Time Significant Journey Journal

1.   Ready yourself for a Fresh encounter with God. Pray and ask God to speak to you. (Psalm 37:7)

Rom - 4:9-12   " In Christ Alone "

2.   Read the Scripture of the Day and prepare to hear a **Fresh Word** from God. (II Timothy 3:16-17)

3.   Respond with the *"Mind of Christ"* by writing down what God has said to you through the Scripture and the devotional thoughts. (Jeremiah 33:3)

- Only faith gives us the right standing w/ God.

4.   Reflect as you *"Experience God"* by listening to His Voice and writing down your prayers and thoughts. (John 16:23)

"religiously right is not right"

★ It is all Christ Alone!

5.   Rely on Jesus to help you live out these truths. (Luke 11:28) Ask, *"Lord, what do you want me to do today?"*   (God's to-do list.)

(Pray for strength as you put on the Full Armor of God.)

Week Four – Day Four

Romans 4:13-17

"God the Promise Keeper"

Has anyone ever made a promise to you that they didn't keep? Have you ever made a promise to someone that you didn't keep? I'm sure many of us could say yes to both questions.

We see something really interesting in this passage. In verse thirteen, Paul noted that God promised Abraham that He would be heir of the world. Now that is a very big promise! But we serve a very big God, Amen! Who is this guy, Abraham, that God would make such a promise? Was he someone super-special that God just had to bless him superabundantly?

God has given us exceeding great and precious promises.

Not necessarily. Abraham was a person that God, by His lavish grace, decided to bless and prosper. The same holds true for us. God has given us, children of God, exceeding great and precious promises. Is it because we deserve it? By no means! It is simply because He loves us. Just as Abraham believed the promises of God, God wants us to place our trust in Him and his Word, also.

Are you sitting on the premises or standing on the promises? Remember that God is not a promise breaker. He is a Promise Keeper. Trust Him today!

2-14-2020

My Quiet Time Significant Journey Journal

1. Ready yourself for a Fresh encounter with God. Pray and ask God to speak to you. (Psalm 37:7)

Rom 4:13-17 "God the Promise Keeper"

2. Read the Scripture of the Day and prepare to hear a **Fresh Word** from God. (II Timothy 3:16-17)

3. Respond with the *"Mind of Christ"* by writing down what God has said to you through the Scripture and the devotional thoughts. (Jeremiah 33:3)

- Abraham received a special promise to be father

"God has given us exceeding great + precious promises."

4. Reflect as you *"Experience God"* by listening to His Voice and writing down your prayers and thoughts. (John 16:23)

"Are you sitting on a promise or standing on a promise? God is not a promise breaker.

5. Rely on Jesus to help you live out these truths. (Luke 11:28) Ask, *"Lord, what do you want me to do today?"* (God's to-do list.)

(Pray for strength as you put on the Full Armor of God.)

Week Four – Day Five

Romans 4:18-22

"Have Faith in God"

Imagine Abram, a 100-year-old man, walking around the neighborhood, telling everyone to start calling him Abraham, telling everyone that he will be a father of many nations. By the way, he didn't have any children. I guess some of his friends thought that he had dementia to some degree. But was Abram, now Abraham, losing his mind? By no means! He just took God at His Word.

The passage tells us that Abraham:

1) "Against hope, he (Abraham) believed..." (vs. 18)

2) "He considered his body to be already dead since he was about 100 years old and also considered the deadness of Sarah's womb without weakening in his faith" (vs. 19)

3) "He did not waiver in unbelief at God's promise." (vs. 20)

In the midst of adverse circumstances, "He was strengthened in his faith and gave glory to God, being fully persuaded that God had the power to do what He promised." How did Abraham become fully persuaded that God could fulfill His promise? In Genesis, chapters 12-20, God came to Abraham in various ways to remind him of His promise. I'm sure that the more Abraham heard the promise, the more he believed. God may not reveal Himself to us like He did to Abraham, but He gave us His Word on which to daily read and meditate.

Are you struggling with doubt or fear? Remind yourself of the promises of God and your faith will be strengthened. "For faith comes by hearing and hearing the words of Christ." (Romans 10:17)

2-17-20

My Quiet Time Significant Journey Journal

1. Ready yourself for a Fresh encounter with God. Pray and ask God to speak to you. (Psalm 37:7)

Romans 4:18-22 "Have faith in God"

2. Read the Scripture of the Day and prepare to hear a **Fresh Word** from God. (II Timothy 3:16-17)

Father of many nations. He did not waiver 22

3. Respond with the *"Mind of Christ"* by writing down what God has said to you through the Scripture and the devotional thoughts. (Jeremiah 33:3)

- Abraham took God at his word.
1. Against hope, he believed
2. Considered dead womb
3. He didn't waiver in unbelief at God's promise

4. Reflect as you *"Experience God"* by listening to His Voice and writing down your prayers and thoughts. (John 16:23)

Remind yourself of God's promises and strengthen your faith. Rom 10:17

5. Rely on Jesus to help you live out these truths. (Luke 11:28) Ask, *"Lord, what do you want me to do today?"* (God's to-do list.)

"Faith comes by hearing + hearing the words of Christ" (Rom 10:17)

(Pray for strength as you put on the Full Armor of God.)

Week Four – Day Six

Romans 4:23-24

"For All People, God Our Righteousness"

Aren't those beautiful words? God didn't just make this righteousness available for Abraham or the Jews. He didn't just make it available for rich people, preachers or very smart people. It is for **all** who believe in Him who raised Jesus our Lord from the dead. The Bible says in Hebrews that Jesus is able to save to the uttermost. One preacher says that Jesus saves from the uttermost to the guttermost! Jesus saves! The Old Testament calls God:

Jehovah-Tsidkenu – God our righteousness

This credit was put into Abrahams account, but also in our account as believers. For all who would believe, God credits it as our righteousness. Take a moment and think about the time in your life when you asked Jesus to be Lord of your life (the time you got saved). Pause and think! Take your time!

Remember how He forgave you and cleansed your life of past sins. Now begin to thank Him for His mercy and grace. When you write down your thoughts and prayers on the next page as you journal today, take your time and pause and think! Praise and Worship your salvation giver. He truly is Jehovah-Tsidkenu. God our righteousness

2-18-20

My Quiet Time Significant Journey Journal

1. **Ready yourself** for a Fresh encounter with God. Pray and ask God to speak to you. (Psalm 37:7)

   For all People, God our Righteousness (Rom 4:23-24)

2. **Read** the Scripture of the Day and prepare to hear a **Fresh Word** from God. (II Timothy 3:16-17)

   Words are not only for him but for us as swell

3. **Respond** with the *"Mind of Christ"* by writing down what God has said to you through the Scripture and the devotional thoughts. (Jeremiah 33:3)

   God made it for all of us not just some.

4. **Reflect** as you *"Experience God"* by listening to His Voice and writing down your prayers and thoughts. (John 16:23)

   Credit was put in our accounts by Jesus

   Remember how God forgave you and cleansed you.

5. **Rely** on Jesus to help you live out these truths. (Luke 11:28) Ask, **"Lord, what do you want me to do today?"** (God's to-do list.)

   Jehova Tsidkenu - God our righteousness

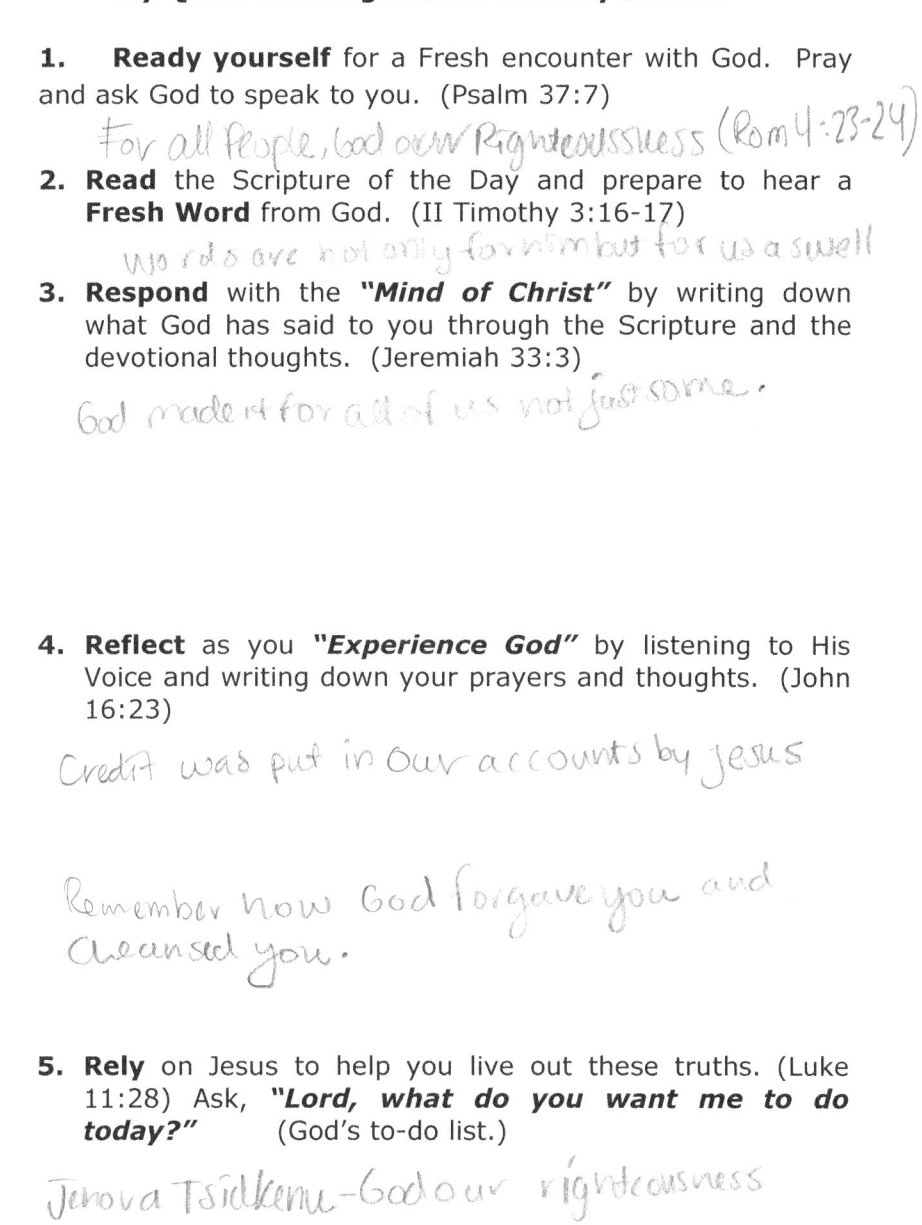

(Pray for strength as you put on the Full Armor of God.)

Week Four – Day Seven

Romans 4:25

"Our Selfless Savior"

The last verse in this chapter gives a short summary of the work of redemption. "He was delivered over to death for our sins and was raised to life for our justification." In this verse, we see the selfless nature of God our Savior.

He died for our sins and was raised to life for our justification. He did not do this for Himself, but for mankind so that we could have access to the very God of the Universe. Praise God forevermore!

Righteousness and Justification are inseparable by the fact that the same Greek word is used for both. But understanding the difference when received and lived out is vital to living the Believing Christian life. By the act of the Grace of God, the righteousness of God, is credited (given) put in the account (imputed) to the believing sinner. Righteousness requires that which is right in character and behavior.

Righteousness is the nature of God Revealed

(mercy and grace demonstrated)

This is the Gospel or "Good News" of Jesus Christ. He died for our sins that we could be declared righteous and enjoy the benefits of being a child of the King! Go and share this Good News! Jesus is our "Selfless Savior"

2-19-20

My Quiet Time Significant Journey Journal

1. Ready yourself for a Fresh encounter with God. Pray and ask God to speak to you. (Psalm 37:7)

Rom 4:25 "Our Selfless Savior"

2. Read the Scripture of the Day and prepare to hear a **Fresh Word** from God. (II Timothy 3:16-17)

He was delivered through death for our sins

3. Respond with the **"Mind of Christ"** by writing down what God has said to you through the Scripture and the devotional thoughts. (Jeremiah 33:3)

The selfless nature of God our Savior.

o Righteousness + Justification same greek word

4. Reflect as you **"Experience God"** by listening to His Voice and writing down your prayers and thoughts. (John 16:23)

Righteousness is the nature of God Revealed.
(mercy + grace demonstrated.)

5. Rely on Jesus to help you live out these truths. (Luke 11:28) Ask, **"Lord, what do you want me to do today?"** (God's to-do list.)

(Pray for strength as you put on the Full Armor of God.)

Week Five – Day One

Romans 5:1

Peace With God

What would be the "heart of the matter" of your faith? What do most people want out of life? Confidence, peace, love, hope, happiness, security, or accomplishment? Can these truly exist without a right standing and peace within ones own being? Paul claims that all these can only exist by our being "justified" (made right in God's sight) by faith in Christ.

Paul begins with the affirmation that we, having been justified, now "have peace with God." Since the words justify and righteousness are two forms of the same root word, we could translate the verse, "having been declared righteous on the principle of faith, we have peace with God through Jesus Christ..." When the question is asked "who shall bring any charge against God's elect?", the answer is wonderful. "It is God who justifies. The source of our justification is God. Instead of being guilty, we are declared righteous. Instead of being condemned, we are acquitted. Instead of being separated, we are joined to the Lord Jesus Christ.

(LET NOT YOUR HEART BE TROUBLED)

This is the heart of the grace of God and the answer to all virtues people are seeking to find. It is the nature of the heart of God to freely offer salvation by the gift of His Son on the cross, shedding His blood, cleansing us from all unrighteousness. The fact remains: God has made peace, and no other peace can be made except that which He has already made.

2-20-20

My Quiet Time Significant Journey Journal

1. Ready yourself for a Fresh encounter with God. Pray and ask God to speak to you. (Psalm 37:7)

Rom. 5:1 "Peace with God"

2. Read the Scripture of the Day and prepare to hear a **Fresh Word** from God. (II Timothy 3:16-17)

We have peace w/ God through our Savior

3. Respond with the *"Mind of Christ"* by writing down what God has said to you through the Scripture and the devotional thoughts. (Jeremiah 33:3)

What people want - confidence, peace, love, hope, happiness, security, accomplish*

"Who shall bring any charge against God's elect?"

4. Reflect as you *"Experience God"* by listening to His Voice and writing down your prayers and thoughts. (John 16:23)

- God has made peace and no other peace can be made except that which He has already made.

5. Rely on Jesus to help you live out these truths. (Luke 11:28) Ask, *"Lord, what do you want me to do today?"* (God's to-do list.)

(Pray for strength as you put on the Full Armor of God.)

Week Five – Day Two

Romans 5:2

Access

"Man's Way to God"

This word access could also be used as "admission" or by the ancient rendering as the "introduction" of one entering the chamber of a royal king. The intended thought was to evoke the believer's high privilege into the throne room of God. In another letter, the Apostle's intent and desire to the Ephesians was the understanding that "In Him (Jesus) we have boldness and access with confidence through faith in Him." (Ephesians 3:12) Remember with peace come access. "For He Himself (Jesus) is our peace, who has made both one, and has broken down the middle wall of separation." (Ephesians 2:14) There is no other entrance, access, but through Jesus. Based on who He is and what He has done for us, let's humbly enter in.

"Direct" Access

What a positive truth is set forth in Scripture when Paul uses the word "into" this grace. Alexander Maclaren beautifully states, "I said that the Apostle was using a metaphor here regarding the grace as being an ample space into which a man was admitted, or we may say that he is thinking of it as a great treasure house. We have the right of entrance there, where, on every side as it were, lies unowned gold and masses of treasure, and we may have just as much or as little as we choose." Oh, what a picture!

Remember as we humbly stand in His presence, Someone, somewhere is also standing together with us. Don't deny such a privilege by taking this access to God lightly. (Psalm 24:3-4)

2-21-20

My Quiet Time Significant Journey Journal

1.   Ready yourself for a Fresh encounter with God. Pray and ask God to speak to you. (Psalm 37:7)

Rom 5:2   "Mans way to God"   Access

2.   Read the Scripture of the Day and prepare to hear a **Fresh Word** from God. (II Timothy 3:16-17)

- Suffering produces perseverance

3.   Respond with the *"Mind of Christ"* by writing down what God has said to you through the Scripture and the devotional thoughts. (Jeremiah 33:3)

Access could be used as "admission"

- Jesus broke down the wall of Seperation

4.   Reflect as you *"Experience God"* by listening to His Voice and writing down your prayers and thoughts. (John 16:23)

Don't take your access to God lightly.

5.   Rely on Jesus to help you live out these truths. (Luke 11:28) Ask, *"Lord, what do you want me to do today?"*   (God's to-do list.)

(Pray for strength as you put on the Full Armor of God.)

Week Five – Day Three

Romans 5:3-5

Does Your Faith Work?

The Apostle Paul now hits right home with the faith. He says, "and not only this…" <u>this</u> being the wonderful doctrine or teaching of justification by faith and our peace with God. He is saying that we put into action that which may seem to be difficult. Think for a minute how rich and peaceful our quiet times can be in the mornings. We say "yes" to Jesus and His promises and truths but go off on our daily journey with all its difficulties and trials thinking "what's wrong?" Paul says nothing is wrong. Everything is right. Your faith has an opportunity to "work." Knowing that it is "God who is working in you both enabling you both to desire and to work out His good purpose." (Philippians 2:13) makes it a little easier too, with a lot less murmurings and complaining with yourself and God. "For we <u>glory</u> or <u>rejoice</u> in <u>tribulation</u>."

(Believe Hope)

A thousand-year-old proverb says, "If it were not for hope, the heart would break." Biblical hope is defined as a strong assurance or expectation of something desired. Hope is desire combined with expectation. Jesus said, "In this world you shall have tribulation, but be of good cheer, I have overcome the world." This hope does not disappoint because the love of God is poured (not sprinkled) in our hearts by the Holy Spirit, which has been given (not earned). This is prayer lived out. Where we stand lived.

My Quiet Time Significant Journey Journal

1. **Ready yourself** for a Fresh encounter with God. Pray and ask God to speak to you. (Psalm 37:7)

2. **Read** the Scripture of the Day and prepare to hear a **Fresh Word** from God. (II Timothy 3:16-17)

3. **Respond** with the *"Mind of Christ"* by writing down what God has said to you through the Scripture and the devotional thoughts. (Jeremiah 33:3)

4. **Reflect** as you *"Experience God"* by listening to His Voice and writing down your prayers and thoughts. (John 16:23)

5. **Rely** on Jesus to help you live out these truths. (Luke 11:28) Ask, **"Lord, what do you want me to do today?"** (God's to-do list.)

(Pray for strength as you put on the Full Armor of God.)

Week Five – Day Four

Romans 5:6-8

Do You Know the Time?
(In Due Season)

I can remember as if it were today when God demonstrated in power His love toward me. It occurred when I asked Him to be by Savior and save me from my sins. It is so humbling to read these passages of Scripture showing me the compelling love of God. It was His truth that set me free and gave me eternity.

These scriptures show us not only the compassion of our Savior but also the actual contrast of human and divine love. Paul says that with human love, it is an extraordinary thing for a man to give his life for a sinner (one who is rebellious, against his Creator, selfish). "But God demonstrates his own love for us in this: while we were still sinners, Christ died for us." My friend, this is not only a miracle to man, but also a demonstration of God proving His unconditional love toward us.

Take time today to recall and meditate on the appointed time in eternity when the Savior came into your heart. Remember: Christ died for you. (Galatians 4:4-7) Realize this awesome gift of eternal life and think about what that can mean to someone else. Practice celebrating this gift and explaining it to someone who needs to know this truth. Let this be your story and song of Praise. And if you do NOT know the time, why not ask Jesus to save you right now! He wants to forgive you and cleanse you and cause you to be born again. Simply ask Jesus to forgive you and come into your life. Tell Him you want to repent of your sins and trust His death as your payment for salvation. And if you do that today, Let your Pastor know!

My Quiet Time Significant Journey Journal

1.   Ready yourself for a Fresh encounter with God. Pray and ask God to speak to you. (Psalm 37:7)

2.   Read the Scripture of the Day and prepare to hear a **Fresh Word** from God. (II Timothy 3:16-17)

3.   Respond with the ***"Mind of Christ"*** by writing down what God has said to you through the Scripture and the devotional thoughts. (Jeremiah 33:3)

4.   Reflect as you ***"Experience God"*** by listening to His Voice and writing down your prayers and thoughts. (John 16:23)

5.   Rely on Jesus to help you live out these truths. (Luke 11:28) Ask, ***"Lord, what do you want me to do today?"***   (God's to-do list.)

(Pray for strength as you put on the Full Armor of God.)

Week Five – Day Five

Romans 5:9-11

Much more!!!

What does it mean, "Much more?" In our Scripture today, this phrase occurs several times. The principle is that God never does anything halfway. Our Lord did not set out to save us and then leave us to our own devices. As the song says, "he did not teach us to swim to let us drown." We are saved from the penalty of sin. But don't stop there. We are also saved from sin's power over us daily.

Reconciled: All God's work for us was done when we were enemies. Every soldier knows what this means. In wartime, enemies are opposite one another. The very atmosphere of death lingers with the enemy. We were the enemies of God but Christ came to change our status as "enemy" to that of "friend." In Eden, God and man faced each other in fellowship. After the fall, sinful man turned from God. The broken union demanded a sacrifice to make things right (atone) in the relationship. God did this at Calvary. Now we must choose to turn back to God. (John 15:13-15)

Once we do, the Lord does so "much more". He restores us! He redeems us! He renews us! He reconciles us! And so very "much more". God wants to give us abundant life and blessings and so "much more." Trust Him today!

My Quiet Time Significant Journey Journal

1.   Ready yourself for a Fresh encounter with God. Pray and ask God to speak to you. (Psalm 37:7)

2.   Read the Scripture of the Day and prepare to hear a **Fresh Word** from God. (II Timothy 3:16-17)

3.   Respond with the *"Mind of Christ"* by writing down what God has said to you through the Scripture and the devotional thoughts. (Jeremiah 33:3)

4.   Reflect as you *"Experience God"* by listening to His Voice and writing down your prayers and thoughts. (John 16:23)

5.   Rely on Jesus to help you live out these truths. (Luke 11:28) Ask, *"Lord, what do you want me to do today?"*   (God's to-do list.)

(Pray for strength as you put on the Full Armor of God.)

Week Five – Day Six

Romans 5:12-14

"Our Way"
Everyone's Way

The command was simple, "You are free to eat from any tree in the garden; but you must not eat from the tree of the knowledge of good and evil." (Genesis 2:16-17) Man was told not to eat the fruit of only one tree. Yet man – the original, the first, with the God-given ability to see, hear, taste, touch, and smell – chose to disobey God's command. With this in mind, the Apostle Paul states the beginning of sin among humanity. With the eating of the fruit, the curse was pronounced upon every man. What is everyone's way? It is declaring our independence of the God who created us with all that we need.

"Charge it to Me"

We are, or were, slaves to sin. The picture of Christ, the Redeemer, that He by the grace of God, should taste death for every man. (Hebrews 2:9) To "impute" is the act of one person adding something good or bad to the account of another person. In today's lesson we read of (1) the imputation of Adam's sin upon the human race, (2) the imputation of the human race's sin upon Christ, and (3) the imputation of God's righteousness upon the believing sinner. So we have learned that sin was added to us, but because of Christ's sacrifice, righteousness (redemption) was added to our account, on account of God's love for us. Thank you Jesus!

My Quiet Time Significant Journey Journal

1. **Ready yourself** for a Fresh encounter with God. Pray and ask God to speak to you. (Psalm 37:7)

2. **Read** the Scripture of the Day and prepare to hear a **Fresh Word** from God. (II Timothy 3:16-17)

3. **Respond** with the *"Mind of Christ"* by writing down what God has said to you through the Scripture and the devotional thoughts. (Jeremiah 33:3)

4. **Reflect** as you *"Experience God"* by listening to His Voice and writing down your prayers and thoughts. (John 16:23)

5. **Rely** on Jesus to help you live out these truths. (Luke 11:28) Ask, **"Lord, what do you want me to do today?"** (God's to-do list.)

(Pray for strength as you put on the Full Armor of God.)

Week Five – Day Seven

Romans 5:15-21

"Someone Totally Different"

Jesus was a carpenter's son, but never had anyone build a kingdom like His. He was one man standing for so many. One day, we will join the angels in the outburst of praise, "The kingdom of the world has become the kingdom of our Lord and of his Christ, and He will reign forever and ever." (Revelation 11:15) The death that began with Adam will end, but the dominion of our Lord will <u>continue</u> forever. "For as in Adam all die; so in Christ all will be made alive." (I Corinthians 15:22)

Much More

Adam's was an act of disobedience and sin. Christ's was an act of obedience and righteousness. He is reigning in life to turn slaves into kings as he takes the child of Adam and lifts him to reign with Christ.

Abundance of Grace

The ancient words transcend the modern description of *abundance*. When we go back to the Latin from which we get our English word, we find it's meaning: "to rise in wars." Sit by the seashore and watch the waves rise again and again, never ceasing. One wave may dash itself on the shore, but as soon as it has spent its force, another sweeps on and on. There is not a need we can think of that His promises do not cover. We have been blessed with <u>all</u> spiritual blessing in the heavenly places with Christ. (Ephesians 1:3)

My Quiet Time Significant Journey Journal

1.   Ready yourself for a Fresh encounter with God. Pray and ask God to speak to you. (Psalm 37:7)

2.   Read the Scripture of the Day and prepare to hear a **Fresh Word** from God. (II Timothy 3:16-17)

3.   Respond with the ***"Mind of Christ"*** by writing down what God has said to you through the Scripture and the devotional thoughts. (Jeremiah 33:3)

4.   Reflect as you ***"Experience God"*** by listening to His Voice and writing down your prayers and thoughts. (John 16:23)

5.   Rely on Jesus to help you live out these truths. (Luke 11:28) Ask, ***"Lord, what do you want me to do today?"***   (God's to-do list.)

(Pray for strength as you put on the Full Armor of God.)

Week Six - Day One

Romans 6:1-2

What "In The World" Am I Doing?

Paul just finishes talking about abounding grace and how much Jesus loved us by dying on the cross. What a gift! But what about the law? It grants knowledge that we are sinning. Would it be true then to say that more law, therefore, requires greater grace? In other words, the greater the amount of sinning, the more grace required?

Should I sin more so that I can experience more grace?? What "in the world" am I doing? Paul emphatically rejects this stance. How could we as believers continue in a sinning mode of life if indeed we are saved? God <u>let</u> His Son be crucified. That pays for the sins of believers. How could we bear that in mind and commit sin?

Yes, we still continue to sin, but the main difference is the Holy Spirit inside the saint granting power over temptations and speaking against the wrong things we are about to do. "God's great love <u>constrains</u> us" in these times. May it never be that we would knowingly sin to experience more grace. A close walk with God lets us hear His voice and lets Him be the Great Shepherd and Provider in our time of need.

My Quiet Time Significant Journey Journal

1. **Ready yourself** for a Fresh encounter with God. Pray and ask God to speak to you. (Psalm 37:7)

2. **Read** the Scripture of the Day and prepare to hear a **Fresh Word** from God. (II Timothy 3:16-17)

3. **Respond** with the *"Mind of Christ"* by writing down what God has said to you through the Scripture and the devotional thoughts. (Jeremiah 33:3)

4. **Reflect** as you *"Experience God"* by listening to His Voice and writing down your prayers and thoughts. (John 16:23)

5. **Rely** on Jesus to help you live out these truths. (Luke 11:28) Ask, **"Lord, what do you want me to do today?"** (God's to-do list.)

(Pray for strength as you put on the Full Armor of God.)

Week Six - Day Two

Romans 6: 3 - 4

Our First Witness

This section of Scripture describes the when and how of a Christian's death to sin. In the New Testament times baptism so closely followed conversion they were considered to be one event. (Acts 2:38) Baptism is not a means by which we enter into a vital faith relationship with Jesus but it is closely associated with faith. Baptism depicts graphically what happens as a result of the Christian's union with Christ. Just as we are united with Adam in our physical birth, we are joined with Christ in our spiritual birth. As we fell into sin and became subject to death in Adam, so we have now died and been raised again with Christ, which baptism symbolizes.

This new life we are to live comes only by the power of the Father. God's glory is His divine excellence, His perfection. Our burial, death, and resurrection via faith in Christ and symbolized by baptism is a manifestation of God's excellence. His perfectly accomplished redemption and witness is through salvation in Christ and baptism.

This outward symbol of inner experience is both literal and figurative. Historians agree that literally believers were dipped or immersed. The figurative is for identification with Christ. If you have been saved and baptized, reflect on your witness as you were baptized before other believers. How closely are you in union with Christ?

My Quiet Time Significant Journey Journal

1. Ready yourself for a Fresh encounter with God. Pray and ask God to speak to you. (Psalm 37:7)

2. Read the Scripture of the Day and prepare to hear a **Fresh Word** from God. (II Timothy 3:16-17)

3. Respond with the ***"Mind of Christ"*** by writing down what God has said to you through the Scripture and the devotional thoughts. (Jeremiah 33:3)

4. Reflect as you ***"Experience God"*** by listening to His Voice and writing down your prayers and thoughts. (John 16:23)

5. Rely on Jesus to help you live out these truths. (Luke 11:28) Ask, ***"Lord, what do you want me to do today?"*** (God's to-do list.)

(Pray for strength as you put on the Full Armor of God.)

Week Six - Day Three

Romans 6:5-10

Know

A Christian is one who follows Christ's great teaching and is one with Christ in a personal relationship. Paul is painting a picture for our minds about this relationship. See in your mind's eye that your old evil-desiring self was nailed to the cross, dealt a fatal wound, and was crushed there. Your sin-loving body is no longer a slave to the old self. See your old self placed into Christ's body on the cross. It died with Him.

Do you want that crucifixion to work for you or do you still want to fight your own battles? This is the paradox. Christ doesn't force His way into your life. He does not walk in and take over. You have a choice. You are no longer under sin's domination, but the choice of which path to follow is still yours.

"Know" that the old self has died in your body. Reckon yourself dead to sin. Believe in your head and your heart that you are alive to God, not alive to sin. Temptation to sin comes, but that sinner's route is no longer the only alternative. Obedience to Christ is now available as an option. "Know" that option, Christian, and choose whom you will serve.

My Quiet Time Significant Journey Journal

1. Ready yourself for a Fresh encounter with God. Pray and ask God to speak to you. (Psalm 37:7)

2. Read the Scripture of the Day and prepare to hear a **Fresh Word** from God. (II Timothy 3:16-17)

3. Respond with the *"Mind of Christ"* by writing down what God has said to you through the Scripture and the devotional thoughts. (Jeremiah 33:3)

4. Reflect as you *"Experience God"* by listening to His Voice and writing down your prayers and thoughts. (John 16:23)

5. Rely on Jesus to help you live out these truths. (Luke 11:28) Ask, *"Lord, what do you want me to do today?"* (God's to-do list.)

(Pray for strength as you put on the Full Armor of God.)

Week Six - Day Four

Romans 6:11

Reckon

Choice is always a part of life. "The only sure things in life are death and taxes" and change. Change is inevitable in a Christian's life or you will grow stagnant in your spiritual development. Every choice you make is turning you toward sin or toward Christ. Which "change" do you want? There is no neutral ground.

This is where reckoning should enter the thoughts of a believer. Since we are always changing, what kind of change do we want? Reckon yourself dead to the ungodly and sinful route and alive to the route to righteousness and Christ. Why are the choices always one or the other and not neutral? The proof lies with the choice offered to everyone (or the lack of choosing), which is to serve Satan or Christ. If you do not believe in Christ, then you are serving Satan. (whether you believe that or not, it is true)

On what have you based your daily circumstantial choices? In a daily walk with the Lord, you absorb and meditate on His Word communicating with Him in prayer. In seeking solutions to both simple and difficult circumstances, you are much more receptive to hearing the truth of a situation when a close personal relationship with the Lord is in tact.

The choices come. Reckon yourself dead to sin and alive to God: "Thy Word is a lamp unto my feet and a light unto my path." And "The steps of a righteous man are ordered by the Lord."

My Quiet Time Significant Journey Journal

1. Ready yourself for a Fresh encounter with God. Pray and ask God to speak to you. (Psalm 37:7)

2. Read the Scripture of the Day and prepare to hear a **Fresh Word** from God. (II Timothy 3:16-17)

3. Respond with the *"Mind of Christ"* by writing down what God has said to you through the Scripture and the devotional thoughts. (Jeremiah 33:3)

4. Reflect as you *"Experience God"* by listening to His Voice and writing down your prayers and thoughts. (John 16:23)

5. Rely on Jesus to help you live out these truths. (Luke 11:28) Ask, *"Lord, what do you want me to do today?"* (God's to-do list.)

(Pray for strength as you put on the Full Armor of God.)

Week Six - Day Five

Romans 6:12-14

Offer

As a Christian you are dead to the old sin-loving self but still have the body of sin that desires its own way. Some believers think that while they may "sin a little" they are still master of a particular habit or practice. It doesn't work that way. You don't master a sin; it masters you. You belong to the power you choose to obey. Unless your faith in Christ is constant and real, sin will still rule your life.

Consider positional, experiential, and ultimate sanctification. Positionally as a Christian we are located in Christ, one with Him, a sanctified saint. Experiential sanctification is having victory over sin on a daily basis. Ultimate sanctification is our heavenly home. How do these tie into the title "offer"?

Verse 13 reflects, "offers yourself to God..." Our position is clearly stated in scripture. We are seated with Christ in the heavenlies. Experientially is where the title "offer" comes into play. Offer the members of your body as instruments of righteousness, not wickedness. Yesterday's lesson reflected choice of sin or Christ. Now, how are your body members going to be used? Offer them to God in righteousness in the circumstances of each action that you do every minute of every day. The choice is yours. Ultimately, then, our Lord will be able to say, "Well done, good and faithful servant..." and welcome us to our heavenly home.

My Quiet Time Significant Journey Journal

1.   Ready yourself for a Fresh encounter with God. Pray and ask God to speak to you. (Psalm 37:7)

2.   Read the Scripture of the Day and prepare to hear a **Fresh Word** from God. (II Timothy 3:16-17)

3.   Respond with the *"Mind of Christ"* by writing down what God has said to you through the Scripture and the devotional thoughts. (Jeremiah 33:3)

4.   Reflect as you *"Experience God"* by listening to His Voice and writing down your prayers and thoughts. (John 16:23)

5.   Rely on Jesus to help you live out these truths. (Luke 11:28) Ask, *"Lord, what do you want me to do today?"*   (God's to-do list.)

(Pray for strength as you put on the Full Armor of God.)

Week Six - Day Six

Romans 6:15-18

Volunteer

The fact that we are saved by grace does not give us reason to sin, but it does give us a reason to obey. This fact of grace comes through the extension of the Father toward us, "...unless the Father who sent me (Christ) draws him" (John 6:44) and He wills that all men would be saved. But we have to voluntarily, accept Christ by free choice. Beyond that comes the voluntary "slave to righteousness". The Christian ought to be as enthusiastic in yielding to the Lord as he was to yielding to sin.

The story of the prodigal son (Luke 15:11-24) shows how far toward slavery a person can go before a crisis point may be reached for a change of heart to occur. The son was slave to sin and finally became a physical slave to pigs before his crisis of belief that turned him back to his father. God allows crisis points to penetrate our bonds and baggage to get us to the point of relying on Him. We then can become a volunteer to righteousness, not to the sin, which can so easily besets us.

Notice that Paul shows a basis for the Romans' turning to righteousness, "wholehearted obedience to the form of teaching which you were entrusted." This obviously shows previous knowledge and learning that gave the Romans a basis for choosing righteousness over sinful ways.

My Quiet Time Significant Journey Journal

1. Ready yourself for a Fresh encounter with God. Pray and ask God to speak to you. (Psalm 37:7

2. Read the Scripture of the Day and prepare to hear a **Fresh Word** from God. (II Timothy 3:16-17)

3. Respond with the *"Mind of Christ"* by writing down what God has said to you through the Scripture and the devotional thoughts. (Jeremiah 33:3)

4. Reflect as you *"Experience God"* by listening to His Voice and writing down your prayers and thoughts. (John 16:23)

5. Rely on Jesus to help you live out these truths. (Luke 11:28) Ask, *"Lord, what do you want me to do today?"* (God's to-do list.)

(Pray for strength as you put on the Full Armor of God.)

Week Six - Day Seven

Romans 6:19-23

Think

"Slavery to righteousness... leads to holiness." Advancing in righteousness is part of the sanctification process. We may choose to advance toward Christ or regress into sin.

When we were leading a life of sin, were there any benefits of a lasting, eternal nature? What would have been the results of having stayed in sin? If you serve a master, you can expect to receive wages. It is the same with God. While sin pays death, righteousness pays holiness and peace with God and eternal life. In the old life we produced fruit that made us ashamed. In the new life in Christ we produce fruit that glorifies God and brings joy to our lives.

This segment of Scripture is also a warning. If the believer refuses to surrender his body to the Lord, but uses its members for sinful purposes, then he is in danger of being disciplined by the Father, and this could mean death. (Hebrews 12:5-11) How grateful I am that the Father drew me toward Him and I chose to follow Jesus as my personal Lord and Savior.

Think on these things: righteousness leads to holiness. Seek first His kingdom... and all these things shall be added to you. Know these truths, reckon them to be true in your life, and then yield yourself to God.

My Quiet Time Significant Journey Journal

1.   Ready yourself for a Fresh encounter with God. Pray and ask God to speak to you. (Psalm 37:7)

2.   Read the Scripture of the Day and prepare to hear a **Fresh Word** from God. (II Timothy 3:16-17)

3.   Respond with the *"Mind of Christ"* by writing down what God has said to you through the Scripture and the devotional thoughts. (Jeremiah 33:3)

4.   Reflect as you *"Experience God"* by listening to His Voice and writing down your prayers and thoughts. (John 16:23)

5.   Rely on Jesus to help you live out these truths. (Luke 11:28) Ask, *"Lord, what do you want me to do today?"*   (God's to-do list.)

(Pray for strength as you put on the Full Armor of God.)

Week Seven - Day One

Romans 7:1-5

Footloose and Fancy Free

In chapter seven, God addresses the Jews specifically because they were steeped in the tradition of the law for centuries. Our Father understands that deeper roots need a little more persuasion to let loose of the soil they have held on to so long. In His love He wants them to have every opportunity to understand they are free! He wisely uses an example in the law to illustrate their freedom from the law to embrace Christ. Paul uses a human example that was common in that day. It all had to do with Jewish Law and Traditions.

Great!! Good for God! Good for the Jewish Christians; but I'm a gentile. We are not Jewish in our beliefs. Yes, but how many of us grow up in the traditions of "religion" to discover God's grace and return to that bondage while waiving the banner of grace? We receive our salvation by grace through faith but we live bound by the old "law" and tradition of what we were taught by others instead of reading God's Word and allowing His Holy Spirit to teach us His Truth. "Therefore, as you have received Christ Jesus the Lord, walk in Him" Col. 2:6. If we received our Salvation by grace through faith; we need to walk by grace in faith! Grace and faith are not a license to sin but rather a freedom to follow Jesus. Don't ever let go of that freedom! Don't let anybody take it from you! Follow the Truths of God's Word. Know where you stand and live in that stance. Read Galatians 5:1. Exercise it today.

My Quiet Time Significant Journey Journal

1.   Ready yourself for a Fresh encounter with God. Pray and ask God to speak to you. (Psalm 37:7)

2.   Read the Scripture of the Day and prepare to hear a **Fresh Word** from God. (II Timothy 3:16-17)

3.   Respond with the ***"Mind of Christ"*** by writing down what God has said to you through the Scripture and the devotional thoughts. (Jeremiah 33:3)

4.   Reflect as you ***"Experience God"*** by listening to His Voice and writing down your prayers and thoughts. (John 16:23)

5.   Rely on Jesus to help you live out these truths. (Luke 11:28) Ask, ***"Lord, what do you want me to do today?"***   (God's to-do list.)

(Pray for strength as you put on the Full Armor of God.)

Week Seven – Day Two

Romans 7:6-13

Freedom with Responsibilities

A father once discussed with his teen-age daughter his hopes for their somewhat distant future. It went something like this...

"I want you to know this will always be your home as long as you choose. There should be no reason for you to be in a hurry to leave home after graduation. Why do most young people want to get out on their own away from Mom and Dad as soon as possible? Usually it is freedom. They want no more rules. I want you to understand that your mother and I have the goal that as we raise you, you will need fewer and fewer rules. Eventually there will be no rules. You won't need them! In essence you will have taken responsibility and established your own *rules* and convictions and won't need ours. You will feel free to live your life and still enjoy the love and security of home."

This is our relationship with Jesus. The law was there to "raise" us to know right and wrong. The Holy Spirit is here that we will desire to live righteously in a loving relationship with Christ. We have the freedom to be us and still enjoy the love and security of our Father. Am I mature enough to handle this freedom responsibly? Sometimes its easier when there are many boundaries. That's what growing up is about isn't it? The boundaries are removed and we have to decide to stay within the lines when the lines have disappeared. It is nice to have a Light to show the way.

My Quiet Time Significant Journey Journal

1.   Ready yourself for a Fresh encounter with God. Pray and ask God to speak to you. (Psalm 37:7)

2.   Read the Scripture of the Day and prepare to hear a **Fresh Word** from God. (II Timothy 3:16-17)

3.   Respond with the *"Mind of Christ"* by writing down what God has said to you through the Scripture and the devotional thoughts. (Jeremiah 33:3)

4.   Reflect as you *"Experience God"* by listening to His Voice and writing down your prayers and thoughts. (John 16:23)

5.   Rely on Jesus to help you live out these truths. (Luke 11:28) Ask, *"Lord, what do you want me to do today?"*   (God's to-do list.)

(Pray for strength as you put on the Full Armor of God.)

Week Seven - Day Three

Romans 7:14-17

Don't Shoot the Messenger
Because You Don't Like the Message

God wants us to understand that sin is our enemy not the law. The law is simply God's messenger to reveal sin. The law did not bring or invent sin, it merely identified sin as sin. As horrible as cancer is, we cannot be angry with the doctor that discovers it. In fact we are grateful when it is discovered in time for treatment to bring the cure. I've been through that time with close friends. Cancer brings such fear, but after two years of a "clean bill of health" after treatment there is such relief and joy.

Sin is a cancer that invades the life of <u>every</u> person. The law was our doctor to reveal to us this cancer that brings death to <u>all</u>. (Rom.3:23 & 6:23) God's word tells us of a horrible truth. All have sinned! All will die condemned unless we recognize this "cancer" in time to apply the cure. Jesus Christ and His death, burial and resurrection is the cure. Jesus is the only cure. (Acts 4:10-12) Think of the law and all scripture as "Dr. Truth". Don't fight or ignore His diagnosis. It would be a fatal mistake. Be thankful that you learned the truth in time to apply the cure.

If you have not been born again, (John 3:1-7) please accept Jesus' cure for your sin today. Repent of your sin and believe in your heart by faith that Jesus can and will give you everlasting life by His authority as the Son of God. Remember, He is the cure. If you have been "cured", give Him the praise for mighty things He has done for you!

P.S. A daily visit with "Dr. Truth" will prove to be very healthy!

My Quiet Time Significant Journey Journal

1. **Ready yourself** for a Fresh encounter with God. Pray and ask God to speak to you. (Psalm 37:7)

2. **Read** the Scripture of the Day and prepare to hear a **Fresh Word** from God. (II Timothy 3:16-17)

3. **Respond** with the *"Mind of Christ"* by writing down what God has said to you through the Scripture and the devotional thoughts. (Jeremiah 33:3)

4. **Reflect** as you *"Experience God"* by listening to His Voice and writing down your prayers and thoughts. (John 16:23)

5. **Rely** on Jesus to help you live out these truths. (Luke 11:28) Ask, *"Lord, what do you want me to do today?"* (God's to-do list.)

(Pray for strength as you put on the Full Armor of God.)

Week Seven - Day Four

Romans 7:14-22

I Have Found the Enemy And He is Me

"But we know that the law is spiritual: but I am of flesh..." (New American Standard) In verse seven man indirectly accuses the law of being sin. The following verses reveal the absurdity of the accusation. Quite the contrary! The law is not the problem, "I" am.

Verse 14 is introducing a reality. Man is flesh. Notice Paul does not say, "I act fleshy". He says that he is flesh. It is not who I am at this point but what I am that is significant. The margin notes in the NIV tell us that "flesh" has been interpreted as "sinful nature". This is because of what we learn in Romans 6 and 7 and other Scripture, i.e. Rom.6:19 - "because of the weakness of your flesh", and Rom.7:18 "For I know that nothing good dwells in me, that is in my flesh..." (NAS) It is the nature of this earthly body to be sinful. Praise God when we leave this world, we will leave this body behind and receive our heavenly body. (1Cor. 15) Until then the battle is on. In any battle it is imperative that you know who the enemy is. Don't despair! We have an awesome ally.

When I was born again the Holy Spirit brought life to my spirit and took up personal residence within. The Holy Spirit of God almighty lives in me!! (1John 4:4) WOW!!! What an ally! Remember the song, Jesus Loves Me? "They (we) are weak but He is strong. Yes, Jesus loves me..." Let Him be your strength in the battle. He's been there, and done that, but has never lost a battle.

My Quiet Time Significant Journey Journal

1. **Ready yourself** for a Fresh encounter with God. Pray and ask God to speak to you. (Psalm 37:7)

2. **Read** the Scripture of the Day and prepare to hear a **Fresh Word** from God. (II Timothy 3:16-17)

3. **Respond** with the ***"Mind of Christ"*** by writing down what God has said to you through the Scripture and the devotional thoughts. (Jeremiah 33:3)

4. **Reflect** as you ***"Experience God"*** by listening to His Voice and writing down your prayers and thoughts. (John 16:23)

5. **Rely** on Jesus to help you live out these truths. (Luke 11:28) Ask, ***"Lord, what do you want me to do today?"*** (God's to-do list.)

(Pray for strength as you put on the Full Armor of God.)

Week Seven - Day Five

Romans 7:18-23

If at First You Don't Succeed...

It's interesting to watch a child learn to walk. He holds mommy's hand and toddles along. Eventually he lets go and one step, two steps... THUMP! He thinks to himself, "Boy that hurt! I'll never try that again." No, not exactly. Mom or Dad picks up the little tike and he tries again; two steps, maybe three...THUMP! Gradually the cute little guy adds more and more steps and less thumps until we can no longer keep up with him. As we grow older we forget that we still go "thump" on occasion. We slip on ice, trip on a step, or for any number of reasons we are still capable of a "thump" now and then.

Our spiritual growth is similar. As new babies in Jesus we may tend to go "thump" easier and more often. And sometimes as we mature we even get going a little faster than our Father desires. Yesterday we identified an enemy that will constantly try to trip us. Though we know we have won the war through Jesus, the flesh will occasionally win a battle. What really gets me is sometimes the battle I lose is the one I hate to lose the most. By no stretch of the imagination is there ever any justification to sin. It is, however, comforting to know we are in good company as the apostle Paul suffered similar losing battles.

What do we do when we have lost a Battle? We do the same as the little guy just learning to walk. We let our "Daddy" dust us off (1John 1:9) and get up and try again. Proverbs 24:16 teaches that a righteous man falls seven times, but gets up seven times. Jerry Falwell has said "you are only a failure when you quit trying." As you mature in Christ, may your "thumps" be fewer. Never quit!!!

My Quiet Time Significant Journey Journal

1. Ready yourself for a Fresh encounter with God. Pray and ask God to speak to you. (Psalm 37:7)

2. Read the Scripture of the Day and prepare to hear a **Fresh Word** from God. (II Timothy 3:16-17)

3. Respond with the *"Mind of Christ"* by writing down what God has said to you through the Scripture and the devotional thoughts. (Jeremiah 33:3)

4. Reflect as you *"Experience God"* by listening to His Voice and writing down your prayers and thoughts. (John 16:23)

5. Rely on Jesus to help you live out these truths. (Luke 11:28) Ask, ***"Lord, what do you want me to do today?"*** (God's to-do list.)

(Pray for strength as you put on the Full Armor of God.)

Week Seven - Day Six

Romans 7:21-25

Sir Isaac Where Are You?

The "law of gravity" was not new or invented by Sir Isaac Newton. He only recognized it and defined it. Gravity is not a "rule" to obey, but a reality. You drop something, it falls: period!

Paul identifies another "law" of reality. It is a spiritual law. Every time there is an opportunity to do good, evil is present to provide it's own opportunity. (v21) It's the law! It is not a pleasant law, but nevertheless an unavoidable reality.

When it comes to laws of nature and spiritual laws we cannot choose do discard them. Ignoring them and pretending they don't exist won't make them go away either. However, we can choose how we will let them affect us. If you see something falling because of gravity you can choose to let it hit you or move. When you have the opportunity to do good, the opportunity to do evil will always be there too. You at least get to choose!! As a Christian you can have victory through Jesus Christ. (v25)

Today you will have choices: good or evil, right or wrong, flesh or spirit, Christ or the world. Choose now before the heat of the battle and let God help you live the right choices when those opportunities come.

My Quiet Time Significant Journey Journal

1.   Ready yourself for a Fresh encounter with God. Pray and ask God to speak to you. (Psalm 37:7)

2.   Read the Scripture of the Day and prepare to hear a **Fresh Word** from God. (II Timothy 3:16-17)

3.   Respond with the *"Mind of Christ"* by writing down what God has said to you through the Scripture and the devotional thoughts. (Jeremiah 33:3)

4.   Reflect as you *"Experience God"* by listening to His Voice and writing down your prayers and thoughts. (John 16:23)

5.   Rely on Jesus to help you live out these truths. (Luke 11:28) Ask, *"Lord, what do you want me to do today?"*   (God's to-do list.)

(Pray for strength as you put on the Full Armor of God.

Week Seven - Day Seven

Romans 7:1-25

Can You Run That By Me Again?

Today's scripture reading serves as a summary of what we have been learning all week. This is such a powerful passage!

There is a continual battle of "tug of war" in the life of a Christian daily. It is a struggle for control. The contestants are your flesh and the Holy Spirit. Your flesh seems to scream out to the mind and heart, "ME! ME! ME! Do what I want!" Of course the desire of the flesh is only evil. (vv19-21) Then there is the other voice. It has been my experience that this voice normally does not choose to scream or yell. The Spirit speaks consistently with the desire to be heard and obeyed. We have the freedom to choose which voice we will listen to and obey.

We have all heard about the "lust" of the flesh, but the Spirit also "lusts". Lust by definition is a "strong desire". God's Spirit within has a strong desire to express His godliness through you. (vv22,23) This "fruit" is evidence to the world of your identity who, or who's you are.

If you consistently obey the desire of the Spirit, the flesh will automatically be denied. When your time is consumed by obeying the Spirit, there is no time left for the flesh. I urge you to memorize verses 22 and 23. Ask God daily to express Himself through you in these nine areas and name them specifically. You may be surprised! There is a bonus! The more you consistently obey the voice of the Spirit, the quieter the flesh becomes. (But he won't go away: sorry)

"Try it! You'll li-i-i-ke it!" I promise.

My Quiet Time Significant Journey Journal

1. Ready yourself for a Fresh encounter with God. Pray and ask God to speak to you. (Psalm 37:7)

2. Read the Scripture of the Day and prepare to hear a **Fresh Word** from God. (II Timothy 3:16-17)

3. Respond with the *"Mind of Christ"* by writing down what God has said to you through the Scripture and the devotional thoughts. (Jeremiah 33:3)

4. Reflect as you *"Experience God"* by listening to His Voice and writing down your prayers and thoughts. (John 16:23)

5. Rely on Jesus to help you live out these truths. (Luke 11:28) Ask, *"Lord, what do you want me to do today?"* (God's to-do list.)

(Pray for strength as you put on the Full Armor of God.)

Week Eight - Day One

Romans 8: 1 - 4

"No Condemnation"

In the first seven chapters of Romans, Paul offers proof of man's depravity and inability to follow the whole law. The law can only define the nature of sin. It had no atoning value.

Christians can sin and make mistakes, and fail; however, for those who are in Christ Jesus, there is no condemnation. Wow, that sounds awesome but remember, there are consequences for stepping outside of God's design for our lives, but there is no condemnation by Him because of Jesus' payment for believers' confessed sin. We may lose fellowship, direction, details, and peace in ourselves, but we will never lose that relationship with our Father and He is always ready to rescue us on His terms.

Having explained man's dilemma Paul now describes the "true peace" giving release from the body of sin. It is really quite simple: Allow the old law to reveal sin, then come to belief in Jesus, and be under the law of the Spirit of life which yields freedom and pardon: **no condemnation.** Jesus has set us free from control by the old nature and if we choose to follow the Spirit of life, it will control, order our steps, and grant life to our path and a lamp unto our feet.

Jesus suffered condemnation for me when He came as a man in the likeness of sinful flesh. How did this propitiation take place? It is God who justifies by His method. Who can condemn the believer? No one. A free gift was given if we take it: peace with God. Oh what a blessing!

My Quiet Time Significant Journey Journal

1.   Ready yourself for a Fresh encounter with God. Pray and ask God to speak to you. (Psalm 37:7)

2.   Read the Scripture of the Day and prepare to hear a **Fresh Word** from God. (II Timothy 3:16-17)

3.   Respond with the *"Mind of Christ"* by writing down what God has said to you through the Scripture and the devotional thoughts. (Jeremiah 33:3)

4.   Reflect as you *"Experience God"* by listening to His Voice and writing down your prayers and thoughts. (John 16:23)

5.   Rely on Jesus to help you live out these truths. (Luke 11:28) Ask, *"Lord, what do you want me to do today?"*   (God's to-do list.)

(Pray for strength as you put on the Full Armor of God.)

Week Eight - Day Two

Romans 8: 5 - 8

What's Your Mindset?

Facts:

Dwell on self = sinful nature mindset.

Dwell on Spirit = life and peace mindset.

Sinful mindset = death (separation from God).

Godly mindset = life (pleasing to God).

What are my thought patterns? Why do I plan a personal and intimate time with God first each day? What happens if I roll out of bed thinking of the myriad "to-do" list without first spiritually seeking God? Answer: Satan gets a "toe hold" on my day. Focus starts on the world and personal agendas.

God promises to speak to me in a manner I can understand, giving direction about what the day will hold. When I begin by offering the day to God and His purposes, that voice is stronger in my ear and mind. A day begins at peace with my Provider and Shepherd. Without Him it's more like opening the door on a closet crammed full. God grants order and peace rather than an avalanche of "things" when I follow Him daily. As you seek first His kingdom and His righteousness "all these things" (needs from the world physically) will be given to you.

What's your mindset? The mind controlled by the Spirit is "life" that is, abundant life and a life pleasing to God.

My Quiet Time Significant Journey Journal

1.   Ready yourself for a Fresh encounter with God. Pray and ask God to speak to you. (Psalm 37:7)

2.   Read the Scripture of the Day and prepare to hear a **Fresh Word** from God. (II Timothy 3:16-17)

3.   Respond with the *"Mind of Christ"* by writing down what God has said to you through the Scripture and the devotional thoughts. (Jeremiah 33:3)

4.   Reflect as you *"Experience God"* by listening to His Voice and writing down your prayers and thoughts. (John 16:23)

5.   Rely on Jesus to help you live out these truths. (Luke 11:28) Ask, *"Lord, what do you want me to do today?"*   (God's to-do list.)

(Pray for strength as you put on the Full Armor of God.)

Week Eight - Day Three

Romans 8: 9 - 11

Where Do I Belong?

This customer was someone special. He entered my consultant firm and sought me out. "I want your full service at my disposal when I need it; here is a down payment that pays for all of your time. Be ready when I call."

"Yes sir," I replied, "But when?" "I'll call soon," he said. I believed he would and I was ready to go. I had earnest money that would last the rest of my life.

Earnest. Down payment. When I believed Jesus to be my Lord and Savior I became "His to command". He gave me the Holy Spirit as my guarantee that I belonged to Him whenever He called.

The Spirit is within. He leads me to all truth. He guides me through life speaking to me as the one He commands. I know he's there, if He weren't, I wouldn't belong to Christ.

Now there's plenty I want to do on my own but that's not the charge that the Special "Customer" paid for. The "other jobs" are dead. I live for His job and that's all I need.

My Quiet Time Significant Journey Journal

1. Ready yourself for a Fresh encounter with God. Pray and ask God to speak to you. (Psalm 37:7)

2. Read the Scripture of the Day and prepare to hear a **Fresh Word** from God. (II Timothy 3:16-17)

3. Respond with the *"Mind of Christ"* by writing down what God has said to you through the Scripture and the devotional thoughts. (Jeremiah 33:3)

4. Reflect as you *"Experience God"* by listening to His Voice and writing down your prayers and thoughts. (John 16:23)

5. Rely on Jesus to help you live out these truths. (Luke 11:28) Ask, *"Lord, what do you want me to do today?"* (God's to-do list.)

(Pray for strength as you put on the Full Armor of God.)

Week Eight - Day Four

Romans 8: 12 - 17

"Obligation and Determination"

My sinful nature is still there alongside the new nature granted by my Lord. I am in a physical body in a physical world of sin with a new nature of the Spiritual World living in me. God has given me very specific instructions that if I feed (figuratively speaking) this Spiritual nature with His Word it will control my fleshly, sinful body nature. But I have an "obligation" to do that. I have to do it to be strong and victorious. But, I am not obligated to feed (again figuratively speaking) this flesh nature with flesh food of sin. I do not need to sin.

So...which one am I feeding? I usually operate my daily schedule according to the one that gets the most time and attention. What is my mindset first thing in the morning? Do I quench myself or the Spirit? "Jesus arose early... and prayed" (Mark 1:35) He fed the Spirit. In many places in the Word Jesus is the model of morning "devotions", starting His day by spending time with His Father. Now as an heir, God is my Father. His Spirit testifies with mine that I am His child. How else should I start the day except by feeding the nature that I love? "The one I feed will dominate." I must be determined that even though I live in a fleshly body, that I will feed my Spirit first and feed it only thus starving my sinful nature.

My Quiet Time Significant Journey Journal

1. Ready yourself for a Fresh encounter with God. Pray and ask God to speak to you. (Psalm 37:7)

2. Read the Scripture of the Day and prepare to hear a **Fresh Word** from God. (II Timothy 3:16-17)

3. Respond with the *"Mind of Christ"* by writing down what God has said to you through the Scripture and the devotional thoughts. (Jeremiah 33:3)

4. Reflect as you *"Experience God"* by listening to His Voice and writing down your prayers and thoughts. (John 16:23)

5. Rely on Jesus to help you live out these truths. (Luke 11:28) Ask, *"Lord, what do you want me to do today?"* (God's to-do list.)

(Pray for strength as you put on the Full Armor of God.)

Week Eight - Day Five

Romans 8: 18 - 27

Deliverance - Future & Now

Creation is suffering, frustrated, in bondage to decay, and in pain. There is a future time when creation will be restored to its original intent; eternal life and fellowship with God.

We in our mortal bodies are experiencing the same thing. Creation had tasted the original intent and now "eagerly awaits" redemption. We also, when born again and sense and experience the blessings of the Holy Spirit, groan inwardly that we have to endure the present trials, temptations, and circumstances. We long for a heavenly home restoring us to eternal fellowship with God.

There is one difference between the lost and the redeemed of God; and that is the internal presence of the Holy Spirit. I know that my soul and body will be redeemed to eternal life. The lost have no such hope or down payment.

The other main difference is that the Spirit intercedes for us. We don't know what to pray but the Spirit does, and according to God's will! He has led us to the truth for our moment-by-moment need. God promises that He's there. He is! God searches our hearts, knows us, and still wants fellowship. We are His children. That is the hope that is within us. We are being delivered day-by-day and live in hope of God's ultimate redemption

My Quiet Time Significant Journey Journal

1.   Ready yourself for a Fresh encounter with God. Pray and ask God to speak to you. (Psalm 37:7)

2.   Read the Scripture of the Day and prepare to hear a **Fresh Word** from God. (II Timothy 3:16-17)

3.   Respond with the *"Mind of Christ"* by writing down what God has said to you through the Scripture and the devotional thoughts. (Jeremiah 33:3)

4.   Reflect as you *"Experience God"* by listening to His Voice and writing down your prayers and thoughts. (John 16:23)

5.   Rely on Jesus to help you live out these truths. (Luke 11:28) Ask, *"Lord, what do you want me to do today?"*   (God's to-do list.)

(Pray for strength as you put on the Full Armor of God.)

Week Eight - Day Six

Romans 8: 28 - 30

Good to Better to Best

The Bible proves that God is ultimately in control of this world and His universe. We sometimes step out on our own and reap consequences for our actions, but we are still not outside of God's control. He can take circumstances and utilize them for His purposes. God causes us to learn and grow for our good to become conformed into the image of Jesus as we love Him. I Corinthians 13 models the love we should have for God and others.

There are three possibilities of results in our walk with God: good, better, and best. What happens as we are being conformed? We experience Jesus, are filled by His Holy Spirit, and then overflow to others, which is a good result. When that happens, witnessing can take place. We are fulfilling God's call to be salt and light and to do our reasonable service for God.

A better result yet is being called and justified. The best result is being glorified. This final stage is firmly grounded in God's set purpose. It is as certain as if it has already happened. This certainty is the hope that I have within that I am His child and am specially being transformed for His service.

What happens when I don't see the good in a circumstance? Trust God. He sees the whole puzzle of my life and how best to live it. He knows how the pieces fit. Also, the circumstances that I encounter are filtered through God's system of approval as part of His role as Shepherd. He has my best interest at heart.

My Quiet Time Significant Journey Journal

1. Ready yourself for a Fresh encounter with God. Pray and ask God to speak to you. (Psalm 37:7)

2. Read the Scripture of the Day and prepare to hear a **Fresh Word** from God. (II Timothy 3:16-17)

3. Respond with the *"Mind of Christ"* by writing down what God has said to you through the Scripture and the devotional thoughts. (Jeremiah 33:3)

4. Reflect as you *"Experience God"* by listening to His Voice and writing down your prayers and thoughts. (John 16:23)

5. Rely on Jesus to help you live out these truths. (Luke 11:28) Ask, *"Lord, what do you want me to do today?"* (God's to-do list.)

(Pray for strength as you put on the Full Armor of God.)

Week Eight - Day Seven

Romans 8: 31 - 39

Conquerors

I cannot read these verses without becoming excited. The main points: "If God be for us, who can be against us?" "(Christ) is also interceding for us." "In all these things (problems of life) we are more than conquerors through Him who loved us."

The Bible does not promise escape from suffering, but believing God's Word in all of Romans 8 shows me that God cares for, loves, is in control of, and is transforming me into the image of His Son.

Try reading these verses again slowly. Soak in them. Meditate on their full meaning, child of God. These fantastic promises are from God who never lies. He keeps His promises to His children.

My Quiet Time Significant Journey Journal

1.   Ready yourself for a Fresh encounter with God. Pray and ask God to speak to you. (Psalm 37:7)

2.   Read the Scripture of the Day and prepare to hear a **Fresh Word** from God. (II Timothy 3:16-17)

3.   Respond with the ***"Mind of Christ"*** by writing down what God has said to you through the Scripture and the devotional thoughts. (Jeremiah 33:3)

4.   Reflect as you ***"Experience God"*** by listening to His Voice and writing down your prayers and thoughts. (John 16:23)

5.   Rely on Jesus to help you live out these truths. (Luke 11:28) Ask, ***"Lord, what do you want me to do today?"***   (God's to-do list.)

(Pray for strength as you put on the Full Armor of God.)

Week Nine – Day One

Romans 9:1-5

Family Choices

Paul is clearly expressing his heart in these verses. There is a strong intensity in his words as he tries to impress upon his readers how genuinely he feels about the condition of his own people. He insists on the truth of his comments in an intimate way. Paul goes so far as to say, "I could almost wish" (or I used to wish) that it was me instead of my people. Paul is hurting for the members of his "Jewish Family" who have chosen to reject the Messiah: the Lord Jesus Christ. He has passion and compassion over the lostness of his family

The same is true of our families I am sure. It is so tough to watch our mothers, our fathers, brothers, or sisters reject the truth that is all around us. "I could almost wish" it was me also. We need to have the same attitude as Paul in an intense desire for their salvation, but at the same time remember it is their choice. God's promise has not failed, but man has failed to believe God's promise of salvation to whoever would believe.

Pray for God to provide the opportunities and convicting circumstances to draw these loved ones unto Himself, never passing up your opportunities to share the gospel with your words and actions. God is sovereign indeed, but His salvation is full of grace and mercy to those who called upon His name and believe in His Word.

My Quiet Time Significant Journey Journal

1. **Ready yourself** for a Fresh encounter with God. Pray and ask God to speak to you. (Psalm 37:7)

2. **Read** the Scripture of the Day and prepare to hear a **Fresh Word** from God. (II Timothy 3:16-17)

3. **Respond** with the ***"Mind of Christ"*** by writing down what God has said to you through the Scripture and the devotional thoughts. (Jeremiah 33:3)

4. **Reflect** as you ***"Experience God"*** by listening to His Voice and writing down your prayers and thoughts. (John 16:23)

5. **Rely** on Jesus to help you live out these truths. (Luke 11:28) Ask, ***"Lord, what do you want me to do today?"*** (God's to-do list.)

(Pray for strength as you put on the Full Armor of God.)

Week Nine – Day Two

Romans 9:6-13

God's Choices (Part I)

Paul now takes his Roman readers through a little ancient history, starting with God's call to Abraham. God decided of His own will to make Abraham the father of blessing. More than one son was born of the old man, but obviously only one of them could be a part of the succession and God decided it would be Isaac. Rebecca, Isaac's wife, became pregnant with twins, and it was clear that only one could be chosen to be in the line of blessing. God chose Jacob rather than Esau. God chose to follow this line through Judah and David until Christ was born. This was God's plan!

The word of God speaks powerfully and clearly about God's complete freedom to act as He chooses. God's choice was a result of his "all-knowing" character, choosing as He saw fit through eternity. We serve a sovereign LORD God.

The result of all this was that there were two kinds of children of Abraham: "natural (fleshly) children," and children of the promise. (Romans 9:8) Paul saw this still operative, as it is even today, that some acknowledge Jesus as the Christ (children of the promise) and others reject Him (natural (fleshly) children). But...simply speaking, "election" is God's choice that "those that accept Jesus Christ are elected (chosen) or are children of the promise. Those that reject Jesus are fleshly, natural children that have elected (chosen) to spend eternity separated from God in hell .

My Quiet Time Significant Journey Journal

1. Ready yourself for a Fresh encounter with God. Pray and ask God to speak to you. (Psalm 37:7)

2. Read the Scripture of the Day and prepare to hear a **Fresh Word** from God. (II Timothy 3:16-17)

3. Respond with the ***"Mind of Christ"*** by writing down what God has said to you through the Scripture and the devotional thoughts. (Jeremiah 33:3)

4. Reflect as you ***"Experience God"*** by listening to His Voice and writing down your prayers and thoughts. (John 16:23)

5. Rely on Jesus to help you live out these truths. (Luke 11:28) Ask, ***"Lord, what do you want me to do today?"*** (God's to-do list.)

(Pray for strength as you put on the Full Armor of God.)

Week Nine – Day Three

Romans 9:6-13

God's Choices (Part II)

Yesterday, we looked at the term "election" to mean that God distinguishes between those who accept Jesus Christ as elected (chosen) or "children of promise," and those who reject Him as fleshly, natural children.

But verse 13 is a tough one to understand. This quote from Malachi 1:2-3 is troublesome, but should be thought of in the context of the "people" of Jacob and Esau, with particular reference to the Edomites refusal to come to Israel's aid at a time of difficulty. The Apostle's choice of this statement should be understood first as a comment on God's attitude to a people, and second in the light of the usage of the word "hate" as a meaning "love less than." (Luke 14:26)

God has made clear choices (elected) that those who accept Jesus Christ as Lord and Savior (Messiah) become His adopted children, (born again by His Spirit) and those who reject Him are not and they choose to spend eternity in hell.

I love all children. I want what is best for all. Yet, those who are my own are loved "naturally" a "little more" and others outside of my family a "little less than."

God's choices are righteous and just and now the choices are ours. We must accept or reject our "election." God chose (elected) us in Christ Jesus and now we must accept or reject His sovereign will. This is God's Plan of Salvation for everyone.

My Quiet Time Significant Journey Journal

1. **Ready yourself** for a Fresh encounter with God. Pray and ask God to speak to you. (Psalm 37:7)

2. **Read** the Scripture of the Day and prepare to hear a **Fresh Word** from God. (II Timothy 3:16-17)

3. **Respond** with the ***"Mind of Christ"*** by writing down what God has said to you through the Scripture and the devotional thoughts. (Jeremiah 33:3)

4. **Reflect** as you ***"Experience God"*** by listening to His Voice and writing down your prayers and thoughts. (John 16:23)

5. **Rely** on Jesus to help you live out these truths. (Luke 11:28) Ask, ***"Lord, what do you want me to do today?"*** (God's to-do list.)

(Pray for strength as you put on the Full Armor of God.)

Week Nine – Day Four

Romans 9:14-16

God's Choices (Part III)

In the extreme Jewish thought, the fact of election for them was an eternal guarantee of blessedness and the rejection of the Gentiles a guarantee of rejection. So for the Jews to be told by Paul that "in Christ" the Gentiles (all people) were being accepted was a national insult. To attribute this freedom for God to choose was an unrighteous act. Paul addresses this conflict. In the touching conversation between God and Moses recorded in Exodus 33:12-33 and quoted in part in Romans by the Apostle, there is clear evidence that God does make choices and is free to deal even with Moses or whoever as He sees fit. And this still is God's plan of salvation that He so loved the world, that whoever believes shall not perish but have His gift of eternal life.

As Leighton Flowers says: "Effectual Salvation is not given because you are from Israel or for that matter in a "Christian home". God's blessings are not always on the grounds of merit, but on the grounds that God considers best. It is not, and "does not, therefore, depend on man's desire or effort, but on God's mercy." In other words all men are "called" (Greek Kaleo) to salvation, but only those who are "called out" (Greek Ekkaleo) (in Christ) receive salvation. "You must be born again!" We must accept (the call) Jesus Christ as Lord of our lives (to be called out).

My Quiet Time Significant Journey Journal

1. **Ready yourself** for a Fresh encounter with God. Pray and ask God to speak to you. (Psalm 37:7)

2. **Read** the Scripture of the Day and prepare to hear a **Fresh Word** from God. (II Timothy 3:16-17)

3. **Respond** with the *"Mind of Christ"* by writing down what God has said to you through the Scripture and the devotional thoughts. (Jeremiah 33:3)

4. **Reflect** as you *"Experience God"* by listening to His Voice and writing down your prayers and thoughts. (John 16:23)

5. **Rely** on Jesus to help you live out these truths. (Luke 11:28) Ask, ***"Lord, what do you want me to do today?"*** (God's to-do list.)

(Pray for strength as you put on the Full Armor of God.)

Week Nine – Day Five

Romans 9:17-18

God's Sovereignty is Illuminated

The Apostle moves quickly to another illustration of the divine freedom to act not only in mercy but also in hardening. Here God's sovereignty (His right to act) is illuminated (shown clearly).

This dramatic story of God's dealings with Pharaoh through Moses is filled with references to "hardening." Repeatedly, Pharaoh hardens his heart until finally God hardens it for him. Instead of destroying this "rejecter of authority" God's sovereignty allows Pharaoh to be raised up in order to show His power.

It would be easy to see that God placed Pharaoh in his internationally visible position so that when his own hard-heartedness came into conflict with God's purpose, he would become an international illustration of the futility of arrogantly opposing the purposes of God.

God does allow things to take place around us to show His power, purpose, and position as a sovereign God of love, mercy and grace. Romans 8:28-29 echoes loudly again in our ears.

My Quiet Time Significant Journey Journal

1.   Ready yourself for a Fresh encounter with God. Pray and ask God to speak to you. (Psalm 37:7)

2.   Read the Scripture of the Day and prepare to hear a **Fresh Word** from God. (II Timothy 3:16-17)

3.   Respond with the *"Mind of Christ"* by writing down what God has said to you through the Scripture and the devotional thoughts. (Jeremiah 33:3)

4.   Reflect as you *"Experience God"* by listening to His Voice and writing down your prayers and thoughts. (John 16:23)

5.   Rely on Jesus to help you live out these truths. (Luke 11:28) Ask, *"Lord, what do you want me to do today?"*   (God's to-do list.)

(Pray for strength as you put on the Full Armor of God.)

Week Nine – Day Six

Romans 9:19-24

God's Consistency is Illustrated

Paul continues in verse 19 to anticipate the obvious response to those who would reason from a human perspective. He then responds with the nature of God's dealings with mankind, rather than the nature of man's involvement in such dealings.

The analogy of the potter and the clay speaks powerfully to the sovereign consistency of God, Who in His glorious power is free to act in the affairs of man. When considering such authority, do we have any real grounds for questioning His wisdom and integrity? Paul is not saying that man is a powerless lump of clay for this would nullify our responsibility. His is illustrating that God is consistent in His choices that those who reject (or harden their hearts like Pharaoh) are subject to His mercy or wrath as He chooses.

The same is applied to Israel in verses 22-24 as Paul illustrates with a powerful "what if."

God is free, Paul asserts, to take the attitudes and actions of this world and show forth "vessels of wrath" or vessels of mercy."

Again, it is God's choice for God is sovereign, but I am so grateful that He allows us to accept this Grace gift by faith.

My Quiet Time Significant Journey Journal

1.   Ready yourself for a Fresh encounter with God. Pray and ask God to speak to you. (Psalm 37:7)

2.   Read the Scripture of the Day and prepare to hear a **Fresh Word** from God. (II Timothy 3:16-17)

3.   Respond with the ***"Mind of Christ"*** by writing down what God has said to you through the Scripture and the devotional thoughts. (Jeremiah 33:3)

4.   Reflect as you ***"Experience God"*** by listening to His Voice and writing down your prayers and thoughts. (John 16:23)

5.   Rely on Jesus to help you live out these truths. (Luke 11:28) Ask, ***"Lord, what do you want me to do today?"***   (God's to-do list.)

(Pray for strength as you put on the Full Armor of God.)

Week Nine – Day Seven

Romans 9:25-33

God's Consistency is Substantiated

Paul closes this deep study of the "Doctrine of Election" by quoting the prophet Hosea. He shows God's ancient commitment to make those who were "not my people" to be accepted. From Isaiah he substantiates the fact that God has previously turned away from His rebellious people, but has always left Himself a "remnant" or a "Seed" by way of promising a brighter day ahead. God's consistency to carry our His promises is maintained.

God is upheld in these thoughts as consistently sovereign in His dealings with man. God works in ways that wonderfully preserve His control, retaining the dignity, which God invested in man when He created him in His own image, while providing the means to recreate him in Christ Jesus our Lord.

The Doctrine of Election found throughout Chapter 9 focuses on "choices." God chose to accept those who accept Jesus Christ as their Lord and to reject those who do not. Now it is our choice to be a part of the chosen. We have been <u>elected</u> by God unto salvation through Jesus Christ our Lord. (John 3:16) Now the choice is ours.

My Quiet Time Significant Journey Journal

1. **Ready yourself** for a Fresh encounter with God. Pray and ask God to speak to you. (Psalm 37:7)

2. **Read** the Scripture of the Day and prepare to hear a **Fresh Word** from God. (II Timothy 3:16-17)

3. **Respond** with the *"Mind of Christ"* by writing down what God has said to you through the Scripture and the devotional thoughts. (Jeremiah 33:3)

4. **Reflect** as you *"Experience God"* by listening to His Voice and writing down your prayers and thoughts. (John 16:23)

5. **Rely** on Jesus to help you live out these truths. (Luke 11:28) Ask, *"Lord, what do you want me to do today?"* (God's to-do list.)

(Pray for strength as you put on the Full Armor of God.)

Week Ten - Day One

Romans 10:1-4

Goal of the Law - Christ

Years ago I was talking with my son after he and his sister had been arguing like brothers and sisters will often do. During our discussion, I said, "We need to be more like Jesus." At this point, my 7-year old began to cry saying, "But Dad, Jesus was perfect; I can't be perfect!" What an excellent illustration for our text today.

He's right; we can't be perfect (righteous) in and of ourselves. Jesus is the end (or goal) of the law for righteousness, meaning our perfection is no longer based on our works but on our believing in His work. We can have a zeal for God and do many good works thinking that in these works we prove our righteousness. However, the righteousness of God is established totally in Christ and our belief in Him. He is the beginning, middle and end of our righteousness and He completed all the work necessary to make us perfect in God's sight on the cross.

You see, God gave us the law to drive us toward Christ (see Galatians 3:24). No man, except Jesus, has ever met the requirements of the law. The more we try to perfect ourselves with good works, the more evident our need for Christ becomes. I think this became clear to my son when we concluded that our good works are not done for us and our perfection, but for others, that Christ might become their salvation also.

My Quiet Time Significant Journey Journal

1. Ready yourself for a Fresh encounter with God. Pray and ask God to speak to you. (Psalm 37:7)

2. Read the Scripture of the Day and prepare to hear a **Fresh Word** from God. (II Timothy 3:16-17)

3. Respond with the **"Mind of Christ"** by writing down what God has said to you through the Scripture and the devotional thoughts. (Jeremiah 33:3)

4. Reflect as you **"Experience God"** by listening to His Voice and writing down your prayers and thoughts. (John 16:23)

5. Rely on Jesus to help you live out these truths. (Luke 11:28) Ask, **"Lord, what do you want me to do today?"** (God's to-do list.)

(Pray for strength as you put on the Full Armor of God.)

Week Ten - Day Two

Romans 10:5-7

Two Ways to Heaven

After I had trusted Christ as my only way of salvation, a friend surprisingly told me that there were two ways to heaven. I quickly rebutted, quoting John 14:6 where Jesus says, "I am the way, the truth and the life; no one comes to the Father but by Me." He jokingly answered, "Yes, that's one way and the other way is to never break God's law and live a perfect, sinless life like Jesus did."

I don't know about you, but I'll choose the John 14:6 way over my friend's way. I can't make it trying to keep the rules of the law, but I can live by faith in Jesus Christ. That's what Paul is saying in verses 5 and 6. If you are going to establish your own righteousness, you must live by the code of the law, never breaking it. Otherwise, you can believe in Jesus, and choose the righteousness based on faith. As Paul continues in verses 6 and 7, he quotes Deuteronomy 30:12-13. This was after God had given the requirements of the law to Israel and before He said, "See, I set before you today life and prosperity, death and destruction." (Deuteronomy 30:15). So, it's simple. We can choose righteousness based on faith in Christ resulting in life, or we can try to establish our own righteousness based on what we do, resulting in death.

That's not a tough decision. What's even better is that God makes this faith simple and easy to find. We don't have to search for it in heaven or dive the depths of the ocean to find it. We don't have to crawl on our knees to Mecca or build a tower of Babel to reach up to heaven. As we'll see tomorrow, it's as close as our own mouth and heart.

My Quiet Time Significant Journey Journal

1. **Ready yourself** for a Fresh encounter with God. Pray and ask God to speak to you. (Psalm 37:7)

2. **Read** the Scripture of the Day and prepare to hear a **Fresh Word** from God. (II Timothy 3:16-17)

3. **Respond** with the *"Mind of Christ"* by writing down what God has said to you through the Scripture and the devotional thoughts. (Jeremiah 33:3)

4. **Reflect** as you *"Experience God"* by listening to His Voice and writing down your prayers and thoughts. (John 16:23)

5. **Rely** on Jesus to help you live out these truths. (Luke 11:28) Ask, *"Lord, what do you want me to do today?"* (God's to-do list.)

(Pray for strength as you put on the Full Armor of God.)

Week Ten - Day Three

Romans 10:8-10

Believe and Confess

The gospel is available to anyone. Today, Paul tells us just how close it is and what to do once we find it. God made it simple - why do we sometimes make things so difficult? In verse 8, Paul quotes from Deuteronomy 30:14. In this Old Testament passage, the "word" is God's word as found in the law. As Paul takes the passage and applies it to the gospel, "the word of faith," we come to understand that it is near us, in our mouth and in our heart.

Now Paul goes on to explain how the mouth and heart work together to produce saving faith. We need to bring our mouth and heart (our total personality, entire being) into agreement so that they say the same thing. Many people give lip service to God, but their hearts are far from Him. Even Jesus said, "Not everyone who says to me 'Lord, Lord,' will enter the kingdom of heaven..." (Matthew 7:21a). So, when you confess that Jesus is Lord, you had better be dead sure your heart is right along with you.

As your heart believes that God raised Christ from the dead, Paul seems to be emphasizing that true belief will change your actions. James said that "...faith without works is dead" (James 2:20). Our faith and actions should work together to make our faith complete (James 2:22). So friend, your mouth and your faith must work together to produce saving faith. In other words, if you're going to work your mouth, be sure you have faith in your heart to go along with it. Salvation involves inward belief as well as outward confession.

My Quiet Time Significant Journey Journal

1. Ready yourself for a Fresh encounter with God. Pray and ask God to speak to you. (Psalm 37:7)

2. Read the Scripture of the Day and prepare to hear a **Fresh Word** from God. (II Timothy 3:16-17)

3. Respond with the *"Mind of Christ"* by writing down what God has said to you through the Scripture and the devotional thoughts. (Jeremiah 33:3)

4. Reflect as you *"Experience God"* by listening to His Voice and writing down your prayers and thoughts. (John 16:23)

5. Rely on Jesus to help you live out these truths. (Luke 11:28) Ask, *"Lord, what do you want me to do today?"* (God's to-do list.)

(Pray for strength as you put on the Full Armor of God.)

Week Ten - Day Four

Romans 10:11-13

Everyone Who Calls...

God's salvation must be open to all people because the one true God created all people. Whether Jew or Greek, black or white, Asian or American, young or old, rich or poor, the salvation by faith we talked of yesterday must be open to "**everyone who**" believes. With this one word, the passage shows the universal character of salvation through Christ Jesus, the only true God, and demonstrates His desire to redeem His creation. "Traditional" (John 3:16) salvation is true even in our scholarly debates over doctrine.

Verse 12 confirms that there is no distinction between any of the 7.6 billion people (in 2018) on this planet – all have sinned and come short of the glory of God. All, if they are to be saved, must come the same way to Christ. You can't come to Him by the Old Testament ritual or by the Mosaic Law. Salvation is offered to all people on the same basis of mercy – by faith.

In verse 13 Paul quotes Joel 2:32 and again emphasizes in the word "**everyone**" the universal nature of salvation. Joel predicted that everyone who calls on the name of the Lord will be saved. Peter saw the fulfillment of this prophecy on the day of Pentecost (Acts 2:21) and it is being fulfilled in the church today. Even at the end of time, the prophecy rings loud and true that God will save many from every tribe and nation and people and language. Just look at Revelation 5:14 and see who is singing a new song around the throne in heaven.

My Quiet Time Significant Journey Journal

1. Ready yourself for a Fresh encounter with God. Pray and ask God to speak to you. (Psalm 37:7)

2. Read the Scripture of the Day and prepare to hear a **Fresh Word** from God. (II Timothy 3:16-17)

3. Respond with the *"Mind of Christ"* by writing down what God has said to you through the Scripture and the devotional thoughts. (Jeremiah 33:3)

4. Reflect as you *"Experience God"* by listening to His Voice and writing down your prayers and thoughts. (John 16:23)

5. Rely on Jesus to help you live out these truths. (Luke 11:28) Ask, *"Lord, what do you want me to do today?"* (God's to-do list.)

(Pray for strength as you put on the Full Armor of God.)

Week Ten - Day Five

Romans 10:14-15

Beautiful Feet

Do you remember when you were first saved? Where did you hear the message? Do you remember who told you the good news? Where was the person from and who sent him? Our passage today gives a sort of recipe of ingredients necessary for salvation. Paul, by means of a series of rhetorical questions, states the conditions necessary (in reverse order) to call on Christ and be saved. Here, "call on Christ" means to repent of your sins and make Him Lord of your life. The ingredients for salvation include (1) a preacher sent from God, (2) proclamation of the message, (3) hearing the message, and (4) believing the message. Now think back to your own salvation experience and see if these ingredients were present when you first believed.

Because all these conditions are necessary for someone to be saved, Paul goes on to make an appeal for preachers. He quotes Isaiah 52:7 which refers to those who bring the exiles the good news of their impending release from captivity in Babylon. We also are called to bring the good news to those in captivity to sin that they too might be freed. I believe that the word "preacher" means anyone who is a witness for Jesus. Many of us Christians are too timid about sharing our faith with others because we don't feel qualified. It doesn't take an expert. Just share what you **do** know! Nowhere in the Bible is it required of a witness that he go to seminary. The only requirement of a witness is a love relationship with Jesus Christ. So set those beautiful feet to walking and speak out! Remember, they can't hear unless someone preaches to them. Are you called to preach?

My Quiet Time Significant Journey Journal

1. **Ready yourself** for a Fresh encounter with God. Pray and ask God to speak to you. (Psalm 37:7)

2. **Read** the Scripture of the Day and prepare to hear a **Fresh Word** from God. (II Timothy 3:16-17)

3. **Respond** with the *"Mind of Christ"* by writing down what God has said to you through the Scripture and the devotional thoughts. (Jeremiah 33:3)

4. **Reflect** as you *"Experience God"* by listening to His Voice and writing down your prayers and thoughts. (John 16:23)

5. **Rely** on Jesus to help you live out these truths. (Luke 11:28) Ask, *"Lord, what do you want me to do today?"* (God's to-do list.)

(Pray for strength as you put on the Full Armor of God.)

Week Ten - Day Six

Romans 10:16-18

Hearing Is Believing

You've heard the familiar saying, "Seeing is believing!" In the Christian faith, blind eyes are made to see. But for salvation, "Hearing is believing!" Paul begins our passage today by quoting Isaiah 53:1, the classic Messianic prophecy given to the nation of Israel. He indicates that not all the Israelites accepted the good news. We know this is still true today. In fact, even among the rest of the human race, Christ said "Enter through the narrow gate. For wide is the gate and broad is the road that leads to destruction, and many enter through it. But small is the gate and narrow the road that leads to life, and only a few find it." (Matthew 7:13-14)

Paul again emphasizes as in Romans 10:14 that saving faith comes from hearing the good news about Jesus. Would you have believed in Jesus Christ if someone had not told you? No! You had to hear it in order to believe it. You see, hearing truly is believing. What a strong motivation for sharing our faith more. Next, Paul quotes Psalm 19:4 as he anticipates the argument that we've all heard many times, "What about the native deep in uncharted jungles who never hears the good news? Will he be saved?" Read all of Psalm 19 and refer back to Romans 1:20. God has made Himself evident with a general revelation through His creation. People will be judged according to their knowledge. Even though we are to go into all the world to preach the gospel, all men already have a general knowledge of God. We are to continue to preach to clarify the details of the gospel. This will not only bring more people into the kingdom of God, but it will create more "preachers" to share the good news.

My Quiet Time Significant Journey Journal

1. **Ready yourself** for a Fresh encounter with God. Pray and ask God to speak to you. (Psalm 37:7)

2. **Read** the Scripture of the Day and prepare to hear a **Fresh Word** from God. (II Timothy 3:16-17)

3. **Respond** with the ***"Mind of Christ"*** by writing down what God has said to you through the Scripture and the devotional thoughts. (Jeremiah 33:3)

4. **Reflect** as you ***"Experience God"*** by listening to His Voice and writing down your prayers and thoughts. (John 16:23)

5. **Rely** on Jesus to help you live out these truths. (Luke 11:28) Ask, ***"Lord, what do you want me to do today?"*** (God's to-do list.)

(Pray for strength as you put on the Full Armor of God.)

Week Ten - Day Seven

Romans 10:19-21

Jealous God, Stubborn People

Have you ever been jealous? I remember in high school when my girlfriend (now my wife) seemed to be paying way too much attention to another friend. What do you think I did in my jealousy? (I wasn't a Christian at the time) You guessed it. I also began paying a lot of attention to another friend of hers. Now, if either one of us had chosen to be stubborn, we may never have gotten back together. However, my jealousy provoked her to jealousy so that she was drawn back to me. We are still together today and have been married for over 40 years. While the example may not be perfect, our God is a jealous God. He wants our attention, our heart. God in His love for Israel wants to provoke them to jealousy so that they will come back to Him. Paul quotes Deuteronomy 32:21 to suggest that God intended to bring understanding about salvation by faith to the Gentiles, upon whom the Jews looked down upon. He suggests that if the Gentiles understand, then the Jews ought also to understand. God used a human emotion to draw His people back to Himself.

He gave us the example of Israel that we might not be stubborn too! Have you believed the message that has been preached to you? In your heart? How long will God hold out his hands to a disobedient and stubborn people? Remember, He is a jealous God and desires your whole heart!

My Quiet Time Significant Journey Journal

1. Ready yourself for a Fresh encounter with God. Pray and ask God to speak to you. (Psalm 37:7)

2. Read the Scripture of the Day and prepare to hear a **Fresh Word** from God. (II Timothy 3:16-17)

3. Respond with the *"Mind of Christ"* by writing down what God has said to you through the Scripture and the devotional thoughts. (Jeremiah 33:3)

4. Reflect as you *"Experience God"* by listening to His Voice and writing down your prayers and thoughts. (John 16:23)

5. Rely on Jesus to help you live out these truths. (Luke 11:28) Ask, *"**Lord, what do you want me to do today?**"* (God's to-do list.)

(Pray for strength as you put on the Full Armor of God.)

Week Eleven – Day One

Romans 11:1-6

The Gratuitous Grace of Our Giving God

Paul continues his teaching to the Gentile Christians in Rome regarding the question of their salvation. He challenges these believers with a question. Since God has granted grace to the Gentiles, has God rejected the Jews? Has God chosen to let one go in order to bless the other with His salvation? No! By no means! Paul shares his personal background to drive home the point. He is 100 percent Israelite – a child of Abraham from the tribe of Benjamin. Yet, like his Roman sisters and brothers, he is a believer saved by grace. By his work and ministry as a Jewish missionary to a Gentile people, Paul is living proof of God's grace and salvation bridging the gap for all who believe. God is not casting away the nation of Israel. Rather God is using their lack of acceptance of Jesus as Messiah to open the door of faith and belief to the Gentiles. A faithful believing remnant remains.

Many times in our spiritual journey, circumstance and isolation leave us feeling that we are standing alone against the world. Like the prophet Elijah in the Old Testament, we cry out, "Lord, I am all alone. I am the only one left who is faithful to you. No one else understands." Then God answers. His confident Word challenges and reminds us that there is a remnant of others faithfully standing with us for Truth, not by any merit or work of our own doing, but only by the gratuitous grace of our giving God!

Am I lonely and feeling isolated? Am I distracted by the cares of the world and daily routine? I will remember Whose I am and look around at those who are standing with me. I will make a list of the "remnant" who influence my faith and give thanks to God and to them for their loving support.

My Quiet Time Significant Journey Journal

1.   Ready yourself for a Fresh encounter with God. Pray and ask God to speak to you. (Psalm 37:7)

2.   Read the Scripture of the Day and prepare to hear a **Fresh Word** from God. (II Timothy 3:16-17)

3.   Respond with the *"Mind of Christ"* by writing down what God has said to you through the Scripture and the devotional thoughts. (Jeremiah 33:3)

4.   Reflect as you *"Experience God"* by listening to His Voice and writing down your prayers and thoughts. (John 16:23)

5.   Rely on Jesus to help you live out these truths. (Luke 11:28) Ask, **"Lord, what do you want me to do today?"**   (God's to-do list.)

(Pray for strength as you put on the Full Armor of God.)

Week Eleven – Day Two

Romans 11:7-10

Majority or Minority

Am I in the majority or the minority when it comes to righteousness before God? Paul tells his Roman readers the majority of Israel tried to obtain righteousness but failed. Instead, righteousness came to the minority, the remnant of believers. Why?

Right standing before God is always sidetracked when my selfish ambitions get in the way. "I can live for God. I can do it. I can make it work." Well, that's what I think. The truth is, "No, I cannot!" God's desire is that I learn to be totally surrendered in heart, soul, mind and strength and dependent upon Him for salvation. Mine is not to strive on my own. To live in my own strength leads to frustration and failure. Trusting in self robs me of knowing God's abundant presence and provision. Trusting in Him leads to a life of rest and peace. My righteousness before God is not based on ritual, habit, heritage or tradition. I depend solely on God's unmerited grace, freely and lovingly given through Jesus Christ my Lord. Building my faith upon any other base leads to a life of striving, hardness of heart, spiritual blindness and clouded vision. These come as the natural consequence of my choosing to reject God's Truth and choosing "to do what is right in my own eyes."

Choked By The World or Yoked With Christ

Where do I stand before God today? Am I with the "majority" – seeking to live my way while being choked by the cares of the world? Or am I with the faithful "minority" – yoked through faith in Christ? The choice is mine.

My Quiet Time Significant Journey Journal

1. Ready yourself for a Fresh encounter with God. Pray and ask God to speak to you. (Psalm 37:7)

2. Read the Scripture of the Day and prepare to hear a **Fresh Word** from God. (II Timothy 3:16-17)

3. Respond with the *"Mind of Christ"* by writing down what God has said to you through the Scripture and the devotional thoughts. (Jeremiah 33:3)

4. Reflect as you *"Experience God"* by listening to His Voice and writing down your prayers and thoughts. (John 16:23)

5. Rely on Jesus to help you live out these truths. (Luke 11:28) Ask, *"Lord, what do you want me to do today?"* (God's to-do list.)

(Pray for strength as you put on the Full Armor of God.)

Week Eleven – Day Three

Romans 11:11-15

Hope for Israel

Since salvation came to the Gentiles by the Jews' rejection of Jesus Christ, is there hope for Israel? Has Israel fallen from grace with no hope for recovery? Paul responds with an emphatic "No." It is the ministry of the believing remnant to live so abundantly in Christ that others become envious and desire to walk with God. People cannot help but see the radiance of God's presence in His saints – in word and in action. By letting Him shine, darkened lives can become enlightened. The hopeful result is that some may be moved to see their need for God's love and come to know Jesus, His grace, and His salvation.

The Ministry of Contrast

Paul never turned his back on his own people. Well acquainted with the Jewish ways, Paul, a self-proclaimed "Pharisee to the Pharisees" hoped to point his people to God's grace through Jesus Christ. In openly sharing the Gospel to the Gentiles, Paul wished to paint a stark contrast between the strict, legalistic "religion" of Israel and the life of grace based upon Jesus Christ as Lord. Paul hoped that through his ministry, the Jewish people would be moved to an envious desire for the abundant life about which he spoke and that doors would be opened for his sharing the Good News with them. The old saying is true: "You may not be able to lead a horse to water, but you can certainly salt his oats."

Am I living for Christ in such a way that others are envious? Is "Christ in me, the hope of glory" making a difference at home, at work, and in my community? Is there any noticeable difference between me and the many others around me who do not know Jesus?

My Quiet Time Significant Journey Journal

1. Ready yourself for a Fresh encounter with God. Pray and ask God to speak to you. (Psalm 37:7)

2. Read the Scripture of the Day and prepare to hear a **Fresh Word** from God. (II Timothy 3:16-17)

3. Respond with the *"Mind of Christ"* by writing down what God has said to you through the Scripture and the devotional thoughts. (Jeremiah 33:3)

4. Reflect as you *"Experience God"* by listening to His Voice and writing down your prayers and thoughts. (John 16:23)

5. Rely on Jesus to help you live out these truths. (Luke 11:28) Ask, *"Lord, what do you want me to do today?"* (God's to-do list.)

(Pray for strength as you put on the Full Armor of God.)

Week Eleven – Day Four

Romans 11:16-21

Words of Warning

Paul now brings his readers to a word of warning. He reminds the Gentile Roman believers that they have come into the family of God only because Israel chose to reject Jesus as Messiah. Because of this, the unbelieving branches of the olive tree (Israel) were broken off and new branches from a wild olive tree (the Gentile believers) were grafted in.

Grafted by Grace

However, this is not a cause for spiritual arrogance or boasting. Rather, it is a caution to all believers to carefully continue walking in obedient faith in view of the awesomeness of God. God, who removed the original branches and grafted new ones in their place, can choose to remove the grafted branches, as well.

Am I full of spiritual pride? Do I look down on others and view myself as spiritually superior? Am I spiritually exclusive? Do I limit God's grace to other people? I humbly give thanks to my gracious God that His grace reaches and includes me and all who will believe.

My Quiet Time Significant Journey Journal

1. **Ready yourself** for a Fresh encounter with God. Pray and ask God to speak to you. (Psalm 37:7)

2. **Read** the Scripture of the Day and prepare to hear a **Fresh Word** from God. (II Timothy 3:16-17)

3. **Respond** with the *"Mind of Christ"* by writing down what God has said to you through the Scripture and the devotional thoughts. (Jeremiah 33:3)

4. **Reflect** as you *"Experience God"* by listening to His Voice and writing down your prayers and thoughts. (John 16:23)

5. **Rely** on Jesus to help you live out these truths. (Luke 11:28) Ask, **"Lord, what do you want me to do today?"** (God's to-do list.)

(Pray for strength as you put on the Full Armor of God.)

Week Eleven – Day Five

Romans 11:22-24

God's Nature

In view of God's grafting the believing Gentiles into his family, Paul turns to two aspects of God's nature – severity (sternness) and kindness.

God's Severity (Sternness)

God is severe in judgment against those who choose to reject Christ and against the sin that results. Willful disobedience separates me from the protection and provision God has in store for His people. In choosing to step outside of His desire for my life, I must suffer the natural consequences of my own actions – my choices – and pay the price for my sins. God stern severity is always to discipline me to obedience, but I must pay the price for my sins. But I am not left without hope.

God's Kindness

God is kind (full of grace and mercy) in His inclusive offering of salvation to all who, in grace, will trust Christ. The claim of Lordship is available to anyone who in faith recognizes their need for God and in repentance trusts in God for salvation. This gracious gift originates in God's desire that none should perish but that all would be drawn into relationship with Him.

God's Grace For All

All people are given the opportunity to turn to God in repentance, in order that God will save – by His marvelous, infinite mercy and grace.

My Quiet Time Significant Journey Journal

1. **Ready yourself** for a Fresh encounter with God. Pray and ask God to speak to you. (Psalm 37:7)

2. **Read** the Scripture of the Day and prepare to hear a **Fresh Word** from God. (II Timothy 3:16-17)

3. **Respond** with the *"Mind of Christ"* by writing down what God has said to you through the Scripture and the devotional thoughts. (Jeremiah 33:3)

4. **Reflect** as you *"Experience God"* by listening to His Voice and writing down your prayers and thoughts. (John 16:23)

5. **Rely** on Jesus to help you live out these truths. (Luke 11:28) Ask, *"Lord, what do you want me to do today?"* (God's to-do list.)

(Pray for strength as you put on the Full Armor of God.)

Week Eleven – Day Six

Romans 11:25-32

Not Ignorant of the Gospel

Paul does not want his readers to be ignorant and uninformed about the grace God has made available to them. This salvation, offered first to the nation of Israel and now to the gentiles, is not for a select few individuals. It is being revealed by God for all to know and understand.

The Awesomeness of God

Jesus Christ came to earth, fully God and fully human. He was tempted in all ways such as we are and yet He triumphed without sin. He gave Himself as a sacrifice for us, paying a debt He did not owe for the debt of sin we could not pay. He offered Himself for both Jews and Gentiles alike, so that whoever believes in Him may have life eternal. Although as humans we cannot fully comprehend the vastness of God's love and grace for us, we can humbly kneel before Him because of His grace and cry "Holy, holy, holy are you, Lord!" How awesome He is!

God's Unchangeable Nature

God's plan is that all of Israel – the seed of the patriarchs Abraham, Isaac and Jacob, and the engrafted Gentile branches – will turn away from godlessness by the forgiveness of sins and through faith in Christ. God's covenant promise is that He will take away their/our sins! This is God's unchangeable nature. God's gift of grace and His call upon the life of the believer are irrevocable.

Do I live as though I believe this?

My Quiet Time Significant Journey Journal

1.   Ready yourself for a Fresh encounter with God. Pray and ask God to speak to you. (Psalm 37:7)

2.   Read the Scripture of the Day and prepare to hear a **Fresh Word** from God. (II Timothy 3:16-17)

3.   Respond with the *"Mind of Christ"* by writing down what God has said to you through the Scripture and the devotional thoughts. (Jeremiah 33:3)

4.   Reflect as you *"Experience God"* by listening to His Voice and writing down your prayers and thoughts. (John 16:23)

5.   Rely on Jesus to help you live out these truths. (Luke 11:28) Ask, ***"Lord, what do you want me to do today?"***   (God's to-do list.)

(Pray for strength as you put on the Full Armor of God.)

Week Eleven – Day Seven

Romans 11:33-36

The Richness of Knowing

As Paul completes this chapter to his Roman sisters and brothers, it is as though he is struck by the wonder of God's love and grace. Paul is overcome by God's gratuitous grace and the fact that he is yoked with Christ in ministry. Paul sees the radiance of God's presence and power at work redeeming the world and bringing it in to relationship with Him. Paul looks at these Romans of faith and through the generations to us and sees God's inclusiveness. God desires that all people should come to know His salvation. Paul recalls God's unchangeable nature. Blessing is heaped upon blessing as Paul sees the awesomeness of God and cries in humble response:

"How deep is the richness of knowing God! How beyond our human understanding is God's nature and God's ways!"

Created, Redeemed, Empowered, Equipped

God has created us in His image and inspired us with His Spirit of life. God has redeemed us and is recreating us through His grace to be members of His Body, the Church. God is empowering and equipping us as His saints for works of service in building His Kingdom on earth as it is in heaven. We are His forever!

Call to mind God's grace and blessings. Remember His wonderful deeds of protection and provision in your life. Give praise to Him and bless His Name.

"For from him and through him and to him are all things. To him be glory forever! Amen."

My Quiet Time Significant Journey Journal

1. **Ready yourself** for a Fresh encounter with God. Pray and ask God to speak to you. (Psalm 37:7)

2. **Read** the Scripture of the Day and prepare to hear a **Fresh Word** from God. (II Timothy 3:16-17)

3. **Respond** with the *"Mind of Christ"* by writing down what God has said to you through the Scripture and the devotional thoughts. (Jeremiah 33:3)

4. **Reflect** as you *"Experience God"* by listening to His Voice and writing down your prayers and thoughts. (John 16:23)

5. **Rely** on Jesus to help you live out these truths. (Luke 11:28) Ask, *"Lord, what do you want me to do today?"* (God's to-do list.)

(Pray for strength as you put on the Full Armor of God.)

Week Twelve - Day One

Romans 12:1-2

In View of God's Mercy

Whenever you see the word "therefore" you always need to ask, "What is it there for?" Many believe Paul is gathering up the first eleven chapters when he says "therefore". The first eleven chapters have told us how we are condemned based on ourselves, but how there is no condemnation for us in Christ Jesus. Jesus has rescued us from eternal condemnation. What great mercy God has lavished on us!

If you were drowning and someone saved you, would you not feel indebted or obligated to that person? But actually our obligation would be to God, who gave the person the ability to save you. The reality for us is that we were drowning in our sin and the Lord Jesus has rescued us!

In view of God's mercy (by the mercies of God), Paul exhorts us to place our total personalities at the disposal of God. If we ever really look at (view) God's mercy, (what He has done for us), how can we not give our lives in service for Him? God's love and mercy compels us to give our bodies as a living and holy sacrifice to Him.

Understanding and receiving the mercy of God gives us the freedom and power to live for God.

My Quiet Time Significant Journey Journal

1. Ready yourself for a Fresh encounter with God. Pray and ask God to speak to you. (Psalm 37:7)

2. Read the Scripture of the Day and prepare to hear a **Fresh Word** from God. (II Timothy 3:16-17)

3. Respond with the *"Mind of Christ"* by writing down what God has said to you through the Scripture and the devotional thoughts. (Jeremiah 33:3)

4. Reflect as you *"Experience God"* by listening to His Voice and writing down your prayers and thoughts. (John 16:23)

5. Rely on Jesus to help you live out these truths. (Luke 11:28) Ask, *"Lord, what do you want me to do today?"* (God's to-do list.)

(Pray for strength as you put on the Full Armor of God.)

Week Twelve - Day Two

Romans 12:1-2 (cont.)

In View of God's Mercy (cont.)

"For you were bought at a price: therefore glorify God in your body." (I Corinthians 6:20)

In much of Paul's writings we see him move from our position in Christ to our practice as believers in Christ. In the first three chapters of Ephesians, we see our position as believers: chosen and sealed (1:3-23), saved by grace (2:1-10), and united as a part of Christ's body (2:11-3:21). Then in chapter four he moves to our practice as believers. "I, therefore, the prisoner of the Lord, entreat you to walk in a manner worthy of the calling with which you have been called." (Ephesians 4:1)

Likewise here in Romans, in view of who God is and what He had done for us, we are exhorted, or urged to present and to yield our bodies, our total personalities. The body is the instrument through which we express ourselves. Our reasonable or rational service to God is to yield our bodies as a living and holy (set apart for God) sacrifice.

We are to stop assuming an outward expression that is patterned after the standards of this world and does not reflect who we are in Christ and what God has done for us. We are to be transformed by the renewing of our minds so that we will be able to know God's will and see that it is good, pleasing and perfect.

My Quiet Time Significant Journey Journal

1. **Ready yourself** for a Fresh encounter with God. Pray and ask God to speak to you. (Psalm 37:7)

2. **Read** the Scripture of the Day and prepare to hear a **Fresh Word** from God. (II Timothy 3:16-17)

3. **Respond** with the *"Mind of Christ"* by writing down what God has said to you through the Scripture and the devotional thoughts. (Jeremiah 33:3)

4. **Reflect** as you *"Experience God"* by listening to His Voice and writing down your prayers and thoughts. (John 16:23)

5. **Rely** on Jesus to help you live out these truths. (Luke 11:28) Ask, *"Lord, what do you want me to do today?"* (God's to-do list.)

(Pray for strength as you put on the Full Armor of God.)

Week Twelve - Day Three

Romans 12:3-8

The Body of Christ

All that we have is what God has given us. We are a chosen people. We are people for whom Christ has died. We are the light of the world and the salt of the earth. We are not these things because of our merit or goodness, but by the grace of God.

Only because of what Christ has done for us (His great love) and Christ in us, are we able to be or do anything. No one is better than anyone else. We are all level at the foot of the cross.

In verses 4 and 5 Paul introduces the great theme of the church as the body of Christ. The church as the body of Christ is to function as a body. Each part of the body is important and is interrelated to the rest of the body. Each part is needed by the body for the body to function as a whole.

God has gifted each believer in different ways. No one has a certain gift because they are better than anyone else, but because the God of grace has chosen to gift us in a certain way. Whatever gift God has given us, we are to use it to build up the body of Christ and to give God glory. So use, or exercise, your gift for Him and His church so that others may come to know Him. Serve God with all that you are and to the best of your ability, with joy!

My Quiet Time Significant Journey Journal

1. **Ready yourself** for a Fresh encounter with God. Pray and ask God to speak to you. (Psalm 37:7)

2. **Read** the Scripture of the Day and prepare to hear a **Fresh Word** from God. (II Timothy 3:16-17)

3. **Respond** with the *"Mind of Christ"* by writing down what God has said to you through the Scripture and the devotional thoughts. (Jeremiah 33:3)

4. **Reflect** as you *"Experience God"* by listening to His Voice and writing down your prayers and thoughts. (John 16:23)

5. **Rely** on Jesus to help you live out these truths. (Luke 11:28) Ask, *"Lord, what do you want me to do today?"* (God's to-do list.)

(Pray for strength as you put on the Full Armor of God.)

Week Twelve - Day Four

Romans 12:9-13

Honoring Others

Let love be without hypocrisy. Don't pat another believer on the back and say something you don't mean. Don't just pretend you love others, *really* love them.

Hate what is wrong or evil and stand on the side of good. Cleave to that which is good. Cleave means to "stick like adhesive tape; to be welded or cemented together with good things." The believer should always be identified with good things rather than shady or questionable practices.

"Show family affection to one another with brotherly love. Outdo one another in showing honor." (Romans 12:10) What would happen if we devoted ourselves to one another? What does it mean to honor someone? To honor means "to place high value on; to treat with respect." Each person with whom we come in contact is someone for whom Christ has died. Let's bring it closer to home. Do you honor your spouse and your children? How about your fellow church members? Do you honor them or do you talk about them?

How can we do these things? Only by drawing close to Christ and allowing Him to work in us. Only by yielding ourselves to God for His service, realizing His love for us.

My Quiet Time Significant Journey Journal

1.   Ready yourself for a Fresh encounter with God. Pray and ask God to speak to you. (Psalm 37:7)

2.   Read the Scripture of the Day and prepare to hear a **Fresh Word** from God. (II Timothy 3:16-17)

3.   Respond with the *"Mind of Christ"* by writing down what God has said to you through the Scripture and the devotional thoughts. (Jeremiah 33:3)

4.   Reflect as you *"Experience God"* by listening to His Voice and writing down your prayers and thoughts. (John 16:23)

5.   Rely on Jesus to help you live out these truths. (Luke 11:28) Ask, *"Lord, what do you want me to do today?"*   (God's to-do list.)

(Pray for strength as you put on the Full Armor of God.)

Week Twelve - Day Five

Romans 12:9-16

Unselfish Love

Paul is getting painfully practical now. You say you are crucified with Christ? You say you have "died to sin and risen again with Christ?" What better way, then, to test all your new powers than to see if you actually can live and love unselfishly. To love others unselfishly and at the same time be concerned with standing up for your rights is a contradiction in terms. You cannot serve God and self. You cannot go around with the Bible in one hand while waving your personal Bill of Rights in the other.

"But so few Christians around my church really show unselfish love. Why should I be the one to start?" Yes, why should you? You probably wouldn't do a very good job of it anyway. People would think you had suddenly gone a little hyper-spiritual or something. You could even lose some social prestige...

There are all kinds of excuses "to not get carried away" with the list of good deeds in Romans 12. But the excuses don't make the standard any less valid. Paul is not nailing up a list of laws that the Christian has to obey without a slip. He is setting up goals at which to aim and set your sights.

Of course you won't do a perfect job of unselfish loving. You may be criticized, even laughed at. But when Paul talks in Romans 12 of honoring others, of never being lax in Christian zeal, of being glad and patient in trouble, of helping others in need, of praying for those who harm you, he is simply putting muscle on the idea of presenting your body as a "living sacrifice". (Romans 12:1)

My Quiet Time Significant Journey Journal

1. Ready yourself for a Fresh encounter with God. Pray and ask God to speak to you. (Psalm 37:7)

2. Read the Scripture of the Day and prepare to hear a **Fresh Word** from God. (II Timothy 3:16-17)

3. Respond with the *"Mind of Christ"* by writing down what God has said to you through the Scripture and the devotional thoughts. (Jeremiah 33:3)

4. Reflect as you *"Experience God"* by listening to His Voice and writing down your prayers and thoughts. (John 16:23)

5. Rely on Jesus to help you live out these truths. (Luke 11:28) Ask, *"Lord, what do you want me to do today?"* (God's to-do list.)

(Pray for strength as you put on the Full Armor of God.)

Week Twelve - Day Six

Romans 12:14-21

Overcome Evil With Good

Bless those who persecute me?

How can I do that? Do I say, "Bless you my child?" I don't think so. To bless can mean, "to speak well of." From the context we see that it is the opposite of curse. To curse can mean, "to invoke evil on a person." It would seem that we are to have God's best in mind for the person. Later on in this chapter we are instructed to overcome evil with good.

Jesus has said, "Love your enemies and pray for those who persecute you, that you may be the sons of your Father in Heaven."

It helps to know that my fight is not against that person. "For our struggle is not against flesh and blood, but against the rulers, against the authorities, against powers of this dark world and against the spiritual forces of evil in the heavenly realms." (Ephesians 6:12)

God desires to minister to all people through us. By God's Spirit we can bless others.

One way to bless others is to meet their needs. "If your enemy is hungry, feed him, if he is thirsty give him something to drink." We can overcome evil with good.

My Quiet Time Significant Journey Journal

1. **Ready yourself** for a Fresh encounter with God. Pray and ask God to speak to you. (Psalm 37:7)

2. **Read** the Scripture of the Day and prepare to hear a **Fresh Word** from God. (II Timothy 3:16-17)

3. **Respond** with the **"Mind of Christ"** by writing down what God has said to you through the Scripture and the devotional thoughts. (Jeremiah 33:3)

4. **Reflect** as you **"Experience God"** by listening to His Voice and writing down your prayers and thoughts. (John 16:23)

5. **Rely** on Jesus to help you live out these truths. (Luke 11:28) Ask, **"Lord, what do you want me to do today?"** (God's to-do list.)

(Pray for strength as you put on the Full Armor of God.)

Week Twelve - Day Seven

Romans 12:14-21 (cont.)

Let the Lord Handle It

We are not responsible for the actions or character of other people. We are only called to love other people.

A friend tells of a lady who had been hurt six years before. During that time she had never forgiven the individual who had sinned against her. Instead, she nursed her grudge, schemed of get-even tactics, and meditated on hatred. Now she was tired all the time, her face was hard and wore a mask of bitterness. She was neurotic. My, was she neurotic. Such negativism and compulsive criticism as you've never seen! But what do you expect with her mind so focused on evil all the time! My friend talked with her. She was a Christian. He suggested she let her debtor loose just as God had let her loose. Finally, the woman decided, "Well, I guess I'll pardon her, but I don't want anything more to do with her!" "Is that how you'd like God to forgive you?" she was asked, *"to pardon you but then have nothing more to do with you?"* She saw the point and forgiveness flowed. This withered woman began to thrive.

Let God take care of people who have hurt you. Loving people doesn't mean we let people keep hurting us. We are called to speak the truth in love. Loving people means we don't take revenge. We need to let God be God. Let Him be the final judge. "If it is possible, as far as it depends on us, let us live at peace with everyone. Overcome evil with good."

My Quiet Time Significant Journey Journal

1. **Ready yourself** for a Fresh encounter with God. Pray and ask God to speak to you. (Psalm 37:7)

2. **Read** the Scripture of the Day and prepare to hear a **Fresh Word** from God. (II Timothy 3:16-17)

3. **Respond** with the *"Mind of Christ"* by writing down what God has said to you through the Scripture and the devotional thoughts. (Jeremiah 33:3)

4. **Reflect** as you *"Experience God"* by listening to His Voice and writing down your prayers and thoughts. (John 16:23)

5. **Rely** on Jesus to help you live out these truths. (Luke 11:28) Ask, *"Lord, what do you want me to do today?"* (God's to-do list.)

(Pray for strength as you put on the Full Armor of God.)

Week Thirteen - Day One

Romans 13:1-14

Citizens of Heaven, Citizens of Earth

Romans chapters 1-11 lays the foundation for us of many doctrinal issues to believe in. We are given doctrines to stand firm in. Romans chapters 12-16 move us into the realm of service through which we live out our beliefs. In Romans 12 we thought about how to live out Truth within the body of Christ and with the lost. And now: Romans 13 leads us toward fleshing out what we believe in submission to the government authorities as well as practical tips in fulfilling the law of love toward our neighbor. Here we stand, Here we live!

God has established three institutions: the home (Genesis 2:18-25), government (Genesis 9:1-19), and the church (Acts 2). We as believers in the Lord Jesus Christ must give priority and submission to these three institutions. Specifically, Paul is writing to the church at Rome, who living at the heart of the empire had not faced any major persecution. Paul knew that submission to Jesus Christ or the emperor would soon become an issue of prioritized loyalty. You see, Christians are first citizens of Heaven, and then citizens of Earth. This gives us a two-fold responsibility with our first loyalty to our Lord in Heaven. Unfortunately, we live in a society where wrong is right and right is wrong. Practically, we must obey God in relation to the issues that boldly contradict God and His Word.

My Quiet Time Significant Journey Journal

1. Ready yourself for a Fresh encounter with God. Pray and ask God to speak to you. (Psalm 37:7)

2. Read the Scripture of the Day and prepare to hear a **Fresh Word** from God. (II Timothy 3:16-17)

3. Respond with the *"Mind of Christ"* by writing down what God has said to you through the Scripture and the devotional thoughts. (Jeremiah 33:3)

4. Reflect as you *"Experience God"* by listening to His Voice and writing down your prayers and thoughts. (John 16:23)

5. Rely on Jesus to help you live out these truths. (Luke 11:28) Ask, ***"Lord, what do you want me to do today?"***   (God's to-do list.)

(Pray for strength as you put on the Full Armor of God)

Week Thirteen - Day Two

Romans 13:1

Prayer: An Attitude of Submission

Two of the greatest ways to live in submission to the governing authorities today are:

1. Abundance of prayer - lift them up and

2. Lack of gossip - don't tear them down.

Actually, those who speak the most gossip against the government speak to God about the government the least in prayer. Can a godly man speak blessings and curses out of the same mouth? Who gives you the right to curse man who is made in the likeness of God? (James 3:8-12)

Prayer for the governing authorities will actually cure the bad mouthing, the slurs, and the negative speech. Paul urges us that entreaties, prayers, petitions, and thanksgivings be made on behalf of all men, for kings and all in authority. (I Timothy 2:1-2) I know with so many differences of opinion that is so hard. As believers we have opinions personally that should be the truths of God specifically, but at times it is hard. We need to practice praying for "all" whether we agree or not, in order for God to speak to us and direct our paths. Will you commit now to a renewed heart and tongue to pray for all men, especially the governing authorities including those you agree and disagree with? Don't lose sight of the fact that even though sin and evil run rampant in our government and society, our God is sovereign and the kings of the earth are in the palm of His hand. The Church must take a stand again for righteousness and truth and live it out daily

My Quiet Time Significant Journey Journal

1.   Ready yourself for a Fresh encounter with God. Pray and ask God to speak to you. (Psalm 37:7)

2.   Read the Scripture of the Day and prepare to hear a **Fresh Word** from God. (II Timothy 3:16-17)

3.   Respond with the *"Mind of Christ"* by writing down what God has said to you through the Scripture and the devotional thoughts. (Jeremiah 33:3)

4.   Reflect as you *"Experience God"* by listening to His Voice and writing down your prayers and thoughts. (John 16:23)

5.   Rely on Jesus to help you live out these truths. (Luke 11:28) Ask, *"Lord, what do you want me to do today?"*   (God's to-do list.)

(Pray for strength as you put on the Full Armor of God.)

Week Thirteen - Day Three

Romans 13:1-4

Pray, Vote and Do Good

Have you ever considered that the opposition and condemnation coming against you at times could be the direct result of sowing it against others? (Romans 13:1-2) We must be careful to do God's will in the midst of a great or a corrupt government. Yesterday, we learned to pray instead of gossip and curse. Today, we must keep in mind that we cannot move or change people or government. Our responsibility is to vote for those who most support the cause of Jesus Christ. We are not to act according to tradition or a party to support our families because that's the way it's always been.

We must remember that it is God who moves and changes people and government. *Praise God* that our prayers move God who moves and changes others. To have no real fear of authority, Paul tells us in verse 36 to do what is good so that we will receive praise from the same.

So pray (seek God for the authorities), vote (for the people of God who most promote the cause of Christ), and do good (remembering Romans 12:21 - "do not be conquered by evil, but conquer evil with good."

My Quiet Time Significant Journey Journal

1. **Ready yourself** for a Fresh encounter with God. Pray and ask God to speak to you. (Psalm 37:7)

2. **Read** the Scripture of the Day and prepare to hear a **Fresh Word** from God. (II Timothy 3:16-17)

3. **Respond** with the *"Mind of Christ"* by writing down what God has said to you through the Scripture and the devotional thoughts. (Jeremiah 33:3)

4. **Reflect** as you *"Experience God"* by listening to His Voice and writing down your prayers and thoughts. (John 16:23)

5. **Rely** on Jesus to help you live out these truths. (Luke 11:28) Ask, ***"Lord, what do you want me to do today?"*** (God's to-do list.)

(Pray for strength as you put on the Full Armor of God.)

Week Thirteen - Day Four

Romans 13:5-7

Respect, Fear, Honor = Value

We must submit to and obey the government not only because of the <u>condemnation</u> that comes from disobedience, but also for the sake of our conscience. We must keep a clean conscience in the four areas mentioned in verse seven. "Pay your obligations to everyone:"

1.) Taxes - levied on persons and property

(Luke 20:22-25)

2.) Tolls (Customs) - levied on imported and

exported goods.

3.) Respect (Fear) - respect of the man and for his office

4.) Honor - because of their faithful devotion

to their task.

Although all of these obligations and offices may be abused, we are to pay high respect to God, not to man. <u>Respect</u> in our society is lost among the judgmental, self-righteous attitudes. We must learn to respect and teach respect to our children, youth and young adults. <u>Respect</u> is the foundation to friendship and trust. Respect, honor, and fear actually stem from the same word, which means, "to value or esteem highly". It is understood that one of the greatest enemies to loving God and loving our neighbor as ourselves is a lack of the value we place upon these people. As Gary Smalley and John Trent share in their book "The Gift of Honor", we can decide - before we put love into action - that a person is of high value. Love for someone often begins to flow once we have made the decision to honor (respect, fear, and value) them.

My Quiet Time Significant Journey Journal

1.   Ready yourself for a Fresh encounter with God. Pray and ask God to speak to you. (Psalm 37:7)

2.   Read the Scripture of the Day and prepare to hear a **Fresh Word** from God. (II Timothy 3:16-17)

3.   Respond with the ***"Mind of Christ"*** by writing down what God has said to you through the Scripture and the devotional thoughts. (Jeremiah 33:3)

4.   Reflect as you ***"Experience God"*** by listening to His Voice and writing down your prayers and thoughts. (John 16:23)

5.   Rely on Jesus to help you live out these truths. (Luke 11:28) Ask, ***"Lord, what do you want me to do today?"***   (God's to-do list.)

(Pray for strength as you put on the Full Armor of God.)

Week Thirteen - Day Five

Romans 13:8-10

Value, Passion, Obedience

Jesus took the Ten Commandments and broke them into two sections. The first four are in relation to God and the second six are in relation to man. Jesus pulled and combined the whole Old Testament, all the prophets and the Ten Commandments, into two responsibilities and commands for us as believers. Matthew 22:37-10 tells us to love God with all we are and love our neighbor as ourselves.

As we discussed yesterday, love for people often begins to flow once we have made the decision to value them. The logical flow seems to be that as we value God and others in our attitude (mind) we then can love them in our actions.

Theologian and lecturer Jack Reeve says that love is two-fold: love is passion and obedience. Obedience without heart-felt affection (passion) leads only to a discipline oriented by works. Passion for Jesus Christ moves us into a realm of desire and "want to" which precedes our "have to" need to obedience.

As we value Jesus Christ in our relationship with Him, He becomes more precious and rare to us. Flowing out of this value will be passion for Jesus which initiates "want to" obedience. Value in the mind (attitude), passion is in the heart (emotions), and obedience is in the will (choices). What is the result of valuing and loving Jesus Christ? Read verses 8-10.

My Quiet Time Significant Journey Journal

1. **Ready yourself** for a Fresh encounter with God. Pray and ask God to speak to you. (Psalm 37:7)

2. **Read** the Scripture of the Day and prepare to hear a **Fresh Word** from God. (II Timothy 3:16-17)

3. **Respond** with the *"Mind of Christ"* by writing down what God has said to you through the Scripture and the devotional thoughts. (Jeremiah 33:3)

4. **Reflect** as you *"Experience God"* by listening to His Voice and writing down your prayers and thoughts. (John 16:23)

5. **Rely** on Jesus to help you live out these truths. (Luke 11:28) Ask, *"Lord, what do you want me to do today?"* (God's to-do list.)

(Pray for strength as you put on the Full Armor of God.)

Week Thirteen - Day Six

Romans 13:8-10

Love Gives - Lust Gets

As we develop value, passion and obedience toward Jesus Christ, the supernatural overflow will be value, passion and obedience toward others. Verse 10 says that love does no wrong to his neighbor. To totally change our world around us, we must begin to live and model the love of God with others. (John 13:34-35) Those of the world cannot function with God's love because it is not in their hearts. God has poured out His love within us through the Holy Spirit whom He has given to us. (Romans 5:5) Keep in mind that lust (covetousness) seeks to get and love chooses to give. Our problem comes in verse 5.

If we:

   commit adultery - we covet another man's wife

   commit murder - we covet for another man's life

   steal - we covet another man's stuff

Therefore, covetousness is a focus on self, getting, and being a taker in life. Love takes the eye off of the self, getting, and taking, and chooses the best for others that are involved because we have chosen to value others. Read the love list in I Corinthians 13:4-8. Here we have the true, pure love of God. Be reminded that only God has this love. It is He who must pour it out into you and through you to others. Become a great lover of Jesus Christ and He will teach you how to love others!

My Quiet Time Significant Journey Journal

1. **Ready yourself** for a Fresh encounter with God. Pray and ask God to speak to you. (Psalm 37:7)

2. **Read** the Scripture of the Day and prepare to hear a **Fresh Word** from God. (II Timothy 3:16-17)

3. **Respond** with the *"Mind of Christ"* by writing down what God has said to you through the Scripture and the devotional thoughts. (Jeremiah 33:3)

4. **Reflect** as you *"Experience God"* by listening to His Voice and writing down your prayers and thoughts. (John 16:23)

5. **Rely** on Jesus to help you live out these truths. (Luke 11:28) Ask, **"Lord, what do you want me to do today?"** (God's to-do list.)

(Pray for strength as you put on the Full Armor of God.)

Week Thirteen - Day Seven

Romans 13:11-14

Put On Jesus with Passion

If you would ever put off the deeds of darkness and put on the armor of light...

If you would ever behave properly before God and others...

If you would ever move away from carousing, darkness, sexual promiscuity, sensuality, strife and jealousy...

You must first be reminded of the solution to putting away the sins and evils of the heart. "What fills your mind's attention has the priority to steal away your heart's affection." What are you feeding your mind? What comes into your mind through the eye-gate and ear-gate comes out through your feelings and choices.

My friend, put on the Lord Jesus Christ! Feed your inner man! Sit with the Son of the Living God – Jesus – and fall in love with Him! Passionate love for Jesus Christ will kill a thousand sins in your life. (1 Peter 4:8) Don't focus on cutting out sins, lusts, deeds of darkness, and fleshy appetites. Turn your eyes, your ears, your mind, your heart, your choices, your body, and your spirit to love Jesus Christ with ALL, in ALL. Oh, may Jesus be the delight of your soul. Ask God daily for a passionate, extravagant, and affectionate love for Jesus.

Put on the Lord Jesus Christ!

My Quiet Time Significant Journey Journal

1. Ready yourself for a Fresh encounter with God. Pray and ask God to speak to you. (Psalm 37:7)

2. Read the Scripture of the Day and prepare to hear a **Fresh Word** from God. (II Timothy 3:16-17)

3. Respond with the *"Mind of Christ"* by writing down what God has said to you through the Scripture and the devotional thoughts. (Jeremiah 33:3)

4. Reflect as you *"Experience God"* by listening to His Voice and writing down your prayers and thoughts. (John 16:23)

5. Rely on Jesus to help you live out these truths. (Luke 11:28) Ask, **"Lord, what do you want me to do today?"** (God's to-do list.)

(Pray for strength as you put on the Full Armor of God.)

Week Fourteen - Day One

Romans 14:1-9

Conviction

In Webster's dictionary, the third definition of the word <u>conviction</u> is "a strong belief".

All of us have strong beliefs about different things. Often our beliefs or opinions may conflict with others beliefs or opinions. This is the case in this scenario that Paul illustrates. Paul says that one man may believe that it is okay to eat anything, while another person believes that it is profitable only to eat certain foods. He goes on to say that one man may believe that one day is more sacred than another, but another man may consider every day alike. (Romans 14:5)

How can we live in peace with brothers and sisters in Christ who have different viewpoints than ours? Paul gives us a solution in verse 3. "The man who eats everything must not look down on him who does not, and the man who does not eat everything must not condemn the man who does, for God has accepted him."

We (the members of the body of Christ) may disagree with each other on this little point or that. However, let us be sure not to condemn one another, for God has accepted each of us.

My Quiet Time Significant Journey Journal

1.   Ready yourself for a Fresh encounter with God. Pray and ask God to speak to you. (Psalm 37:7)

2.   Read the Scripture of the Day and prepare to hear a **Fresh Word** from God. (II Timothy 3:16-17)

3.   Respond with the ***"Mind of Christ"*** by writing down what God has said to you through the Scripture and the devotional thoughts. (Jeremiah 33:3)

4.   Reflect as you ***"Experience God"*** by listening to His Voice and writing down your prayers and thoughts. (John 16:23)

5.   Rely on Jesus to help you live out these truths. (Luke 11:28) Ask, ***"Lord, what do you want me to do today?"***   (God's to-do list.)

(Pray for strength as you put on the Full Armor of God.)

Week Fourteen - Day Two

Romans 14:10-12

Why Do You Judge Your Brother?

There are a lot of things that were consistent throughout the life of Paul. One of them was this: he was not afraid to hit people between the eyes with the truth (in love). Here he asks two questions that expose something that is lodged in the hearts of the Romans. "Why do you judge your brother? Why do you look down on your brother?"

Not only did those Christians have this issue in their lives, Christians today must deal with it as well. We need to ask the Lord Jesus a tough question. "Lord, am I judgmental and critical?" If so then we must ask, "Why?" (Trust me, Jesus will be honest with you!)

Usually judgmentalism and criticism grow out of the soil of pride and self-righteousness. These kinds of people often see the sins of others but fail to recognize their own sins. (Matthew 7:1-4)

Remember, it was God's amazing grace that saved wretches like us!

My Quiet Time Significant Journey Journal

1.   Ready yourself for a Fresh encounter with God. Pray and ask God to speak to you. (Psalm 37:7)

2.   Read the Scripture of the Day and prepare to hear a **Fresh Word** from God. (II Timothy 3:16-17)

3.   Respond with the *"Mind of Christ"* by writing down what God has said to you through the Scripture and the devotional thoughts. (Jeremiah 33:3)

4.   Reflect as you *"Experience God"* by listening to His Voice and writing down your prayers and thoughts. (John 16:23)

5.   Rely on Jesus to help you live out these truths. (Luke 11:28) Ask, **"Lord, what do you want me to do today?"**   (God's to-do list.)

(Pray for strength as you put on the Full Armor of God.)

Week Fourteen - Day Three

Romans 14:10-12

Jesus the Judge

The position of Judge belongs to Jesus! "For we will all stand before God's judgment seat... so then each of us will give an account of himself to God." (Romans 14:12)

2 Corinthians 5:10 says, "For we must all appear before the judgment seat of Christ, that each one may receive what is due him for the things done while in the body whether good or bad."

Further study of these two passages would reveal that this particular judgment discussed here is for Christians, not for lost sinners. (The Bible does mention another judgment for those who died without Christ.) The judgment mentioned in these verses is not an issue of salvation, for salvation is by faith in Christ, not by works. (Ephesians 2:8-9) Paul is saying there will come a day when each believer's life of service will be under review.

This is a sobering fact because the one conducting the examination is omniscient. He knows everything about us. He knows our thoughts and the intents of our hearts. These are some of the things that give Him the rightful place as judge.

Let us spend more time seeking intimacy with Jesus rather than criticizing and judging our brothers and sisters. **Let Jesus be the Judge!**

My Quiet Time Significant Journey Journal

1. Ready yourself for a Fresh encounter with God. Pray and ask God to speak to you. (Psalm 37:7)

2. Read the Scripture of the Day and prepare to hear a **Fresh Word** from God. (II Timothy 3:16-17)

3. Respond with the *"Mind of Christ"* by writing down what God has said to you through the Scripture and the devotional thoughts. (Jeremiah 33:3)

4. Reflect as you *"Experience God"* by listening to His Voice and writing down your prayers and thoughts. (John 16:23)

5. Rely on Jesus to help you live out these truths. (Luke 11:28) Ask, **"Lord, what do you want me to do today?"** (God's to-do list.)

(Pray for strength as you put on the Full Armor of God.)

Week Fourteen - Day Four

Romans 14:13-16

Stumbling Blocks or Stepping Stones

Paul says we are to "...make up your minds not to put any stumbling blocks (something a person trips over) or obstacles (a trap or snare, anything that would lead another to sin) in your brothers way." Paul is encouraging a change in mindset. He says to stop judging one another and instead make a decision to help one another.

Is this your mindset? Are you seeking to be a stepping-stone of faith for your brother or are you a stumbling block? Is your attitude one that says, "This is what I'm going to do or say and if you can't deal with that then you need to get over it!" Or is it, "I know I have freedom in Christ to do or say that, but if those things will cause my brother or sister to stumble, I will make the adjustments Jesus tells me to make in order to help my brother or sister."

"Lord, teach me how to meet people where they are, to help take them to where you want them to go (which is Christ's' likeness).

My Quiet Time Significant Journey Journal

1.   Ready yourself for a Fresh encounter with God. Pray and ask God to speak to you. (Psalm 37:7)

2.   Read the Scripture of the Day and prepare to hear a **Fresh Word** from God. (II Timothy 3:16-17)

3.   Respond with the *"Mind of Christ"* by writing down what God has said to you through the Scripture and the devotional thoughts. (Jeremiah 33:3)

4.   Reflect as you *"Experience God"* by listening to His Voice and writing down your prayers and thoughts. (John 16:23)

5.   Rely on Jesus to help you live out these truths. (Luke 11:28) Ask, ***"Lord, what do you want me to do today?"***   (God's to-do list.)

(Pray for strength as you put on the Full Armor of God.)

Week Fourteen - Day Five

Romans 14:17-18

What Really Matters?

Sometimes we focus on the wrong things. We tend to focus on what kind of music is being played in our Sunday services, what version of the Bible we should read, should we clap our hands, lift our hands, or keep them in our pockets. Although these things are important to some, they don't make up the kingdom of God.

Paul had to remind the Romans that the kingdom of God is not about eating certain foods, worshipping on certain days, or drinking certain things. The kingdom of God is about righteousness, peace and joy in the Holy Spirit.

Our focus should first of all be on Jesus and on developing intimacy with Him. We also should focus on helping others to experience the righteousness, peace and joy of the kingdom of God. This is what really matters.

My Quiet Time Significant Journey Journal

1. **Ready yourself** for a Fresh encounter with God. Pray and ask God to speak to you. (Psalm 37:7)

2. **Read** the Scripture of the Day and prepare to hear a **Fresh Word** from God. (II Timothy 3:16-17)

3. **Respond** with the ***"Mind of Christ"*** by writing down what God has said to you through the Scripture and the devotional thoughts. (Jeremiah 33:3)

4. **Reflect** as you ***"Experience God"*** by listening to His Voice and writing down your prayers and thoughts. (John 16:23)

5. **Rely** on Jesus to help you live out these truths. (Luke 11:28) Ask, ***"Lord, what do you want me to do today?"*** (God's to-do list.)

(Pray for strength as you put on the Full Armor of God.)

Week Fourteen - Day Six

Romans 14:18-21

Peace and Edification

Paul tells the Romans (and us) to do something that is consistent with Whom we belong (the Prince of Peace) and who we are (peace makers) (Matthew 5:9). First of all, he says to make every effort that leads to peace with one another.

We are not to be people who stir up problems and demand our rights with one another. We are to strive to live in peace with each other. He also says to edify or build up one another.

Is there someone with whom you are at odds? Have you honestly made every effort to do what leads to peace in this relationship? This doesn't mean comprising the Word of God, but it means doing everything Jesus has commanded you to do regarding your relationships. Are you building up people around you with encouraging words or does negativity and criticism often flow from your lips?

Remember, we are to be peacemakers and edifiers.

My Quiet Time Significant Journey Journal

1. Ready yourself for a Fresh encounter with God. Pray and ask God to speak to you. (Psalm 37:7)

2. Read the Scripture of the Day and prepare to hear a **Fresh Word** from God. (II Timothy 3:16-17)

3. Respond with the *"Mind of Christ"* by writing down what God has said to you through the Scripture and the devotional thoughts. (Jeremiah 33:3)

4. Reflect as you *"Experience God"* by listening to His Voice and writing down your prayers and thoughts. (John 16:23)

5. Rely on Jesus to help you live out these truths. (Luke 11:28) Ask, *"Lord, what do you want me to do today?"* (God's to-do list.)

(Pray for strength as you put on the Full Armor of God.)

Week Fourteen - Day Seven

Romans 14:22-23

When In Doubt, Seek God!

Bill and Bob (both of whom were Christians) were sitting on the porch enjoying each other's company.

Bill asked Bob, "Bob, is it wrong for me to chew tobacco?" Bob responded, "Well, it depends on whether or not the Holy Spirit convicts you of it."

"How do I know if the Holy Spirit is convicting me of it or not?" Bill asked. Bob responded, "You'll know when you start asking questions like, 'Is it wrong for me to chew tobacco?'"

The issue here is not whether tobacco chewing is a sin. The issue is faith versus doubt. Paul says "...everything that is not from a conviction (faith) is sin." (Romans 14:23) There is so many "gray areas" in our world today. As a believer let's don't try to see what we can get away with. Let's walk so close to Jesus that we want to please Him first and not be a stumbling block to others. Let's don't demand our own way, but seek God's way.

As Christians we ought to seek God's will and seek to be pleasing in His sight. If there is even a question in our hearts of whether or not what we are doing is pleasing to God, we should not proceed any further.

When in doubt, seek God!

My Quiet Time Significant Journey Journal

1. **Ready yourself** for a Fresh encounter with God. Pray and ask God to speak to you. (Psalm 37:7)

2. **Read** the Scripture of the Day and prepare to hear a **Fresh Word** from God. (II Timothy 3:16-17)

3. **Respond** with the *"Mind of Christ"* by writing down what God has said to you through the Scripture and the devotional thoughts. (Jeremiah 33:3)

4. **Reflect** as you *"Experience God"* by listening to His Voice and writing down your prayers and thoughts. (John 16:23)

5. **Rely** on Jesus to help you live out these truths. (Luke 11:28) Ask, ***"Lord, what do you want me to do today?"*** (God's to-do list.)

(Pray for strength as you put on the Full Armor of God.)

Week Fifteen – Day One

Romans 15:1-6

"Some Are Weak, Some Are Strong"

This Scripture is extremely important to the church of today. To better understand why, let's draw an analogy.

Think of your favorite <u>team sport</u>. (football, basketball, baseball, etc.) Now, think of your favorite <u>team</u>. (If it's anything besides the Carolina Panther or the Charlotte Hornets, we'll pray for you.) Now, think about the <u>individual players</u> on the team. Are they all the same size? Do the players all play the same positions? Is the talent of skill level the same for all the players? *Of course not.* You cannot have a team of all quarterbacks or forwards or catchers. On every team, someone has to be the biggest, fastest and strongest, and someone has to be the smallest, slowest and weakest. All these strengths and weaknesses are spread throughout the players and each are both good and bad at any given moment. That's <u>why</u> it is called a team. Everyone different – some stronger and some weaker – yet working toward the common goal, <u>together!</u> Verse 6 even says, "with a unified mind and voice." *Unity!*

No matter how good a running back may be, he cannot block for himself. He must have the help of someone stronger than he. Once he is in the clear, a big strong blocker would only slow him down. His speed then becomes his strength. Working with one another's strengths and weaknesses, the team moves forward.

How have you helped the team today?

My Quiet Time Significant Journey Journal

1. Ready yourself for a Fresh encounter with God. Pray and ask God to speak to you. (Psalm 37:7)

2. Read the Scripture of the Day and prepare to hear a **Fresh Word** from God. (II Timothy 3:16-17)

3. Respond with the *"Mind of Christ"* by writing down what God has said to you through the Scripture and the devotional thoughts. (Jeremiah 33:3)

4. Reflect as you *"Experience God"* by listening to His Voice and writing down your prayers and thoughts. (John 16:23)

5. Rely on Jesus to help you live out these truths. (Luke 11:28) Ask, *"Lord, what do you want me to do today?"* (God's to-do list.)

(Pray for strength as you put on the Full Armor of God.)

Week Fifteen – Day Two

Romans 15:7-13

"Accepting Our Differences"

Paul goes on to talk more about acceptance. He is speaking primarily about the acceptance of Jews and Gentiles of one another. Paul says that acceptance of one another brings praise to God. Why so much about acceptance?

Our particular church is made up of many different backgrounds and denominations. Can you see how there might be some differences of opinion at church? What Paul is saying is focus on what you have in common. Do we all believe Jesus Christ is the Way, the Truth and the Life? Yes. Do we all agree it is important that we lead others to a saving knowledge of Jesus Christ? Yes. These are things we have in common. We can always find areas in which we do not agree. I may not necessarily agree with the way one of my close friends raises their children. Should I stop associating with them because of a difference of opinion? Certainly not. We agree to disagree and move on.

Paul is encouraging the Gentile to praise the Lord. He is being inclusive of those not like the Jews. He is encouraging everyone to focus on the common ground. Is the glass half full or half empty? It is amazing how a different perspective can affect a situation. Which part are you focusing on?

My Quiet Time Significant Journey Journal

1. Ready yourself for a Fresh encounter with God. Pray and ask God to speak to you. (Psalm 37:7)

2. Read the Scripture of the Day and prepare to hear a **Fresh Word** from God. (II Timothy 3:16-17)

3. Respond with the *"Mind of Christ"* by writing down what God has said to you through the Scripture and the devotional thoughts. (Jeremiah 33:3)

4. Reflect as you *"Experience God"* by listening to His Voice and writing down your prayers and thoughts. (John 16:23)

5. Rely on Jesus to help you live out these truths. (Luke 11:28) Ask, *"Lord, what do you want me to do today?"* (God's to-do list.)

(Pray for strength as you put on the Full Armor of God.)

Week Fifteen – Day Three

Romans 15:14=16

"Presentation is Everything"

Paul is a master of words. Remember that he is addressing this letter to Roman Christians, a pretty scary thing to be at that day and time. He wants to remind them to continue in Godliness. Paul is in jail at this point and is probably lacking some of the modern conveniences of the day. He probably sleeps on a hard floor, spends most, if not all of his time in chains, and probably isn't being over-fed. Given this particular set of circumstances, what would your frame of mind be? A little cranky? That's probably a reasonable conclusion. <u>Paul has some strong words to say, but look at what he says first.</u>

He tells them he is <u>convinced</u> they are full of goodness, have a good knowledge of the Word, and are able to teach one another. He built them up. He focused on the positive. He saw their glass as being half-full, not half-empty. His admonition is given in love. It is an <u>encouragement</u> of what they are doing right.

Someone once said: "If you have a big, juicy steak that is fit for a king, but serve it on a garbage can lid, who wants it? No one. Presentation is everything."

We all disagree on something. True Christian maturity presents these differences in love and works through them.

My Quiet Time Significant Journey Journal

1. Ready yourself for a Fresh encounter with God. Pray and ask God to speak to you. (Psalm 37:7)

2. Read the Scripture of the Day and prepare to hear a **Fresh Word** from God. (II Timothy 3:16-17)

3. Respond with the *"Mind of Christ"* by writing down what God has said to you through the Scripture and the devotional thoughts. (Jeremiah 33:3)

4. Reflect as you *"Experience God"* by listening to His Voice and writing down your prayers and thoughts. (John 16:23)

5. Rely on Jesus to help you live out these truths. (Luke 11:28) Ask, **"Lord, what do you want me to do today?"** (God's to-do list.)

(Pray for strength as you put on the Full Armor of God.)

Week Fifteen – Day Four

Romans 15:17-22

"Who Gets the Credit?"

Paul is very careful about what he takes credit for. He says he will only talk about that which the Lord has accomplished through him. There are signs and miracles along the say to point to Jesus. He is very clear that it is not he who has done these things, but Christ working through him. He does state very clearly that he has made a choice and that choice is to proclaim Jesus wherever He was not being proclaimed. Paul wants it to be clear that Christianity is not a religion to be mingled with another teaching. He says he does not want to build on someone else's foundation. He wants there to be no mistake that he is preaching on behalf of Jesus Christ.

Has anyone outside of Jesus suffered as much for the gospel of Christ as Paul? Probably not. Yet, he takes no credit for the things that are God's doing. He has pure motives! Can we say that? After we've worked hard for the Lord, do we want to take the credit for the results? Someone to notice what we've done? No matter how big or small, it is always a God thing.

Paul was sold out to God. He even denied his desire to see friends so the gospel could be preached. That's commitment. How's yours?

My Quiet Time Significant Journey Journal

1.   Ready yourself for a Fresh encounter with God. Pray and ask God to speak to you. (Psalm 37:7)

2.   Read the Scripture of the Day and prepare to hear a **Fresh Word** from God. (II Timothy 3:16-17)

3.   Respond with the *"Mind of Christ"* by writing down what God has said to you through the Scripture and the devotional thoughts. (Jeremiah 33:3)

4.   Reflect as you *"Experience God"* by listening to His Voice and writing down your prayers and thoughts. (John 16:23)

5.   Rely on Jesus to help you live out these truths. (Luke 11:28) Ask, *"Lord, what do you want me to do today?"*   (God's to-do list.)

(Pray for strength as you put on the Full Armor of God.)

Week Fifteen – Day Five

Romans 15:23-28

"Bound and Determined"

Paul's single goal in life was to share the gospel message of the Christ who changed his life. Paul's ultimate goal was to get to Spain. He was able to keep that long-term goal while working toward shorter-term goals. Working from city to city, he was able to see most of, if not all of Asia Minor evangelized. This does not mean everyone accepted Christ, just that they heard the gospel preached. Now that's determination. Do we have that same determination today to share with our neighbors and friends?

Paul wants to go personally to Jerusalem because at one time in his life he had been their greatest persecutor. He wanted to make things right once and for all.

Paul encourages the churches of Achaia and Macedonia to help support the believers in Jerusalem. He suggests that because the gospel began in Jerusalem, the other churches owe a debt to that church – bearing one another's burdens – the weak helping the strong. Sound familiar?

Finally, Paul wants to see to it that the offering gets where it is supposed to go. He is a man who finished what he started. He says so in II Tim. 4:7 – "I have fought a good fight, I have finished my course, I have kept the faith." He has done all he set out to do. Can we say the same?

My Quiet Time Significant Journey Journal

1. Ready yourself for a Fresh encounter with God. Pray and ask God to speak to you. (Psalm 37:7)

2. Read the Scripture of the Day and prepare to hear a **Fresh Word** from God. (II Timothy 3:16-17)

3. Respond with the *"Mind of Christ"* by writing down what God has said to you through the Scripture and the devotional thoughts. (Jeremiah 33:3)

4. Reflect as you *"Experience God"* by listening to His Voice and writing down your prayers and thoughts. (John 16:23)

5. Rely on Jesus to help you live out these truths. (Luke 11:28) Ask, *"Lord, what do you want me to do today?"* (God's to-do list.)

(Pray for strength as you put on the Full Armor of God.)

Week Fifteen – Day Six

Romans 15:29-33

The Darkest Night is Just Before the Dawn

Paul says he will arrive in the fullness of the blessing of Christ. Does this mean he will arrive with no hardships and with Christ smiling over his shoulder? Hardly. Often when we are in the middle of hardship or pain and suffering, we think we must be out of the will of God. Usually, just the opposite is the case. It is <u>because</u> we are in the will of God that we endure these hardships – to build character.

Paul begs the people to pray. Not just any old prayer, but to agonize with him in prayer. He has two specific requests. First, that he should be delivered from the religious leaders in Judea who were trying to kill him and second, that the church in Jerusalem would receive the offering he was to bring. (They might be hesitant since the offering was coming from Gentiles.)

He concludes his prayers that he might join them with joy (in spite of all he has been through) and that he might be refreshed. He was <u>expecting</u> God to answer the prayers of the people and he was already looking forward to the welcome home party. He had his eyes set on things beyond his circumstances. His eyes were focused on the finish line.

Paul ends with a statement that only a giant in the faith could make. "The God of peace be with you all." Is this the same man who has been in prison, in chains, in storms, in shipwrecks, running for his life? How can he make a statement that God is a God of peace? By faith he makes it. What is our testimony about the God we serve?

My Quiet Time Significant Journey Journal

1.   Ready yourself for a Fresh encounter with God. Pray and ask God to speak to you. (Psalm 37:7)

2.   Read the Scripture of the Day and prepare to hear a **Fresh Word** from God. (II Timothy 3:16-17)

3.   Respond with the ***"Mind of Christ"*** by writing down what God has said to you through the Scripture and the devotional thoughts. (Jeremiah 33:3)

4.   Reflect as you ***"Experience God"*** by listening to His Voice and writing down your prayers and thoughts. (John 16:23)

5.   Rely on Jesus to help you live out these truths. (Luke 11:28) Ask, ***"Lord, what do you want me to do today?"***   (God's to-do list.)

(Pray for strength as you put on the Full Armor of God.)

Week Fifteen – Day Seven

Romans 15

Review

Let's sum up what we've seen this week. In verses 1-13 we studied about those among us who are weaker. Never make the assumption that because someone has been a believer in Jesus Christ for many years that they are strong in their faith. If they have not studied the Word in order to know God, they are weak. Likewise, do not assume someone who has been a Christian for only a short time is necessarily weak. If they are s student of the Word, they are growing stronger each day and may be stronger than those who have believed for many years. We are to encourage those that are weak and help them along.

In verses 14-22, Paul dealt with acceptance of one another. He spoke mainly of Jew and Gentile. We speak of those of other denominations or those within our denomination who simply believe something slightly different than us. We must remember that none of us are perfect. None of us have all the answers. This is why love for one another is what holds us together. We can agree to disagree in love.

Lastly, we see that Paul did not give up. He pressed on until he reached his destination. He set a goal out in front of him and he worked incessantly toward it. He was purpose driven. He wanted to affect people for the gospel of Christ and nothing would stand in his way. But on his way, we see that he ministered to all kinds of people. He was inclusive. After all this, he had the faith and fortitude to wish the people peace. What a man of God! What an example for each of us!

My Quiet Time Significant Journey Journal

1. **Ready yourself** for a Fresh encounter with God. Pray and ask God to speak to you. (Psalm 37:7)

2. **Read** the Scripture of the Day and prepare to hear a **Fresh Word** from God. (II Timothy 3:16-17)

3. **Respond** with the *"Mind of Christ"* by writing down what God has said to you through the Scripture and the devotional thoughts. (Jeremiah 33:3)

4. **Reflect** as you *"Experience God"* by listening to His Voice and writing down your prayers and thoughts. (John 16:23)

5. **Rely** on Jesus to help you live out these truths. (Luke 11:28) Ask, ***"Lord, what do you want me to do today?"*** (God's to-do list.)

(Pray for strength as you put on the Full Armor of God.)

Week Sixteen - Day One

Romans - Review Chapters 1-15

Review - Part I

How we stand and How we live! Paul covers it all in this book of Romans. Throughout the book he has talked about judgment, God's ways, God's purpose, faith, obedience, the Holy Spirit, sin, death, resurrection, the church, etc., and some clear statements on salvation. Our doctrinal stance and our practical lifestyle.

All these things are very important, but let's be sure that we clearly understand this salvation Paul speaks of.

... Who needs God's salvation? Everyone!

(Romans 3:23 - <u>all</u> have sinned)

... What does this <u>salvation</u> cost? Nothing!

(Romans 6:23 - Eternal life is a <u>free gift</u> of God.)

... Why did God give us this gift?

(Romans 5:8 - Because of <u>love</u> Jesus paid the death

penalty for our sins.)

In chapter 1 verse 16 Paul says, "<u>For I am not ashamed of the gospel</u>, because it is God's power for salvation to everyone who believes: first to the Jew, and also to the Greek."

Salvation is not limited to any group of people. (Romans 9:15-18) So <u>exactly</u>, <u>precisely</u> what do we do to be a part of God's plan for world salvation? **"Confess Jesus as Lord and believe God raised him from the dead."** (Romans 10:9-10)

My Quiet Time Significant Journey Journal

1. Ready yourself for a Fresh encounter with God. Pray and ask God to speak to you. (Psalm 37:7)

2. Read the Scripture of the Day and prepare to hear a **Fresh Word** from God. (II Timothy 3:16-17)

3. Respond with the ***"Mind of Christ"*** by writing down what God has said to you through the Scripture and the devotional thoughts. (Jeremiah 33:3)

4. Reflect as you ***"Experience God"*** by listening to His Voice and writing down your prayers and thoughts. (John 16:23)

5. Rely on Jesus to help you live out these truths. (Luke 11:28) Ask, ***"Lord, what do you want me to do today?"*** (God's to-do list.)

(Pray for strength as you put on the Full Armor of God.)

Week Sixteen - Day Two

Romans - Review Chapters 1-15

Review - Part II

Salvation... Yes... Then what?

So, your salvation is right. You have accepted Jesus as your Savior. You now know, through your faith that you are going to Heaven. The indwelling Spirit of God dwells within you. You have confessed (agreed with God) your sins and repented of them. You know where you *"stand"* and can tell others.

Is there more? *Yes!* <u>Now you must let Jesus be your Lord!</u> How do you do this? Simply by turning over the rule of your life to Jesus. You see, you have a wonderful personal teacher - the Holy Spirit of God. (John 14:26) He will guide you to apply Biblical principles according to God's will, revealing God, His purposes and His ways to you. The Holy Spirit honors and uses God's Word in speaking to you and your life.

If you are one of those who have been frustrated in your Christian experiences, realizing that something is missing, knowing God has a more abundant life for you, try letting Him be Lord in your *"life."* Let the Spirit of God bring you into an intimate relationship with the Father.

Anything or anyone who takes your focus off God can become your lord and prevent you from allowing God's love to flow through your life.

So now you know! Today, at this moment, let God control you life and work through you to establish His kingdom on Earth.

Now the God of peace be with you all. Amen. (Romans 15:33)

My Quiet Time Significant Journey Journal

1.   Ready yourself for a Fresh encounter with God. Pray and ask God to speak to you. (Psalm 37:7)

2.   Read the Scripture of the Day and prepare to hear a **Fresh Word** from God. (II Timothy 3:16-17)

3.   Respond with the *"Mind of Christ"* by writing down what God has said to you through the Scripture and the devotional thoughts. (Jeremiah 33:3)

4.   Reflect as you *"Experience God"* by listening to His Voice and writing down your prayers and thoughts. (John 16:23)

5.   Rely on Jesus to help you live out these truths. (Luke 11:28) Ask, ***"Lord, what do you want me to do today?"***   (God's to-do list.)

(Pray for strength as you put on the Full Armor of God.)

Week Sixteen - Day Three

Romans 16:1-2

The Trusted One

Paul's "support group" or "help mates" appear to be his loyal friends and supporters. All were believers living in Rome or they were believers who were with the Apostle Paul. He expresses a mutual love and tender affection for these people, which was a contradiction of Roman philosophy and practice.

Phoebe is the first believer mentioned. As a Gentile, Paul entrusts her with the important task of delivering the Epistle to the Romans. She is called a "servant of the church," which means she was possibly a deaconess (Greek - diakonas). Paul refers to Phoebe as a sister, a saint, and a helper, and warmly commends her. (Romans 16:1) She was a true, dedicated servant, ready to do God's will.

How about your heart? Is it a servant's heart or do you pick and choose what <u>you</u> want to do (self-centeredness)? Are you willing to run errands or do you insist on sitting at the "head table"?

Have you noticed that some people <u>demand to be served</u> rather than <u>to serve</u>? Phoebe could have chosen to attend a luncheon she had been invited to, or planned to play golf, or she just might have wanted to rest. She chose to be a servant.

"For even the Son of Man did not come to be served, but to serve, and give his life as a ransom for many." (Mark 10:45)

My Quiet Time Significant Journey Journal

1. **Ready yourself** for a Fresh encounter with God. Pray and ask God to speak to you. (Psalm 37:7)

2. **Read** the Scripture of the Day and prepare to hear a **Fresh Word** from God. (II Timothy 3:16-17)

3. **Respond** with the *"Mind of Christ"* by writing down what God has said to you through the Scripture and the devotional thoughts. (Jeremiah 33:3)

4. **Reflect** as you *"Experience God"* by listening to His Voice and writing down your prayers and thoughts. (John 16:23)

5. **Rely** on Jesus to help you live out these truths. (Luke 11:28) Ask, *"Lord, what do you want me to do today?"* (God's to-do list.)

(Pray for strength as you put on the Full Armor of God.)

Week Sixteen - Day Four

Romans 16:3-16

Partners - The Body of Christ

In these verses, Paul is calling the roll and sending greetings to his loved ones. What a conglomerate! It is clear that some of the believers are of Jewish origin, that some of them knew Christ before Paul, that some were slaves, others from the household of Herod, that some had shared prison cells with Paul, and others had cared for him and even "mothered him".

Priscilla and Aquila risked their lives for Paul. Numerous people are commended for their "labor". They are described as "beloved". Paul repeatedly uses the expression "in the Lord" to identify the bond that holds them together.

At this time, the local church met in private homes. (Acts 12:12; Colossians 4:15) These were **T**ender **L**oving **C**are groups that Christ put together to carry on His work bringing together Gentiles and Jews, men and women, slaves and free, to share spiritual and material blessing. (Romans 15:26-27)

What a beautiful picture.

"People Helping People Know the Love of Jesus."

My Quiet Time Significant Journey Journal

1. Ready yourself for a Fresh encounter with God. Pray and ask God to speak to you. (Psalm 37:7)

2. Read the Scripture of the Day and prepare to hear a **Fresh Word** from God. (II Timothy 3:16-17)

3. Respond with the *"Mind of Christ"* by writing down what God has said to you through the Scripture and the devotional thoughts. (Jeremiah 33:3)

4. Reflect as you *"Experience God"* by listening to His Voice and writing down your prayers and thoughts. (John 16:23)

5. Rely on Jesus to help you live out these truths. (Luke 11:28) Ask, *"Lord, what do you want me to do today?"* (God's to-do list.)

(Pray for strength as you put on the Full Armor of God.)

Week Sixteen - Day Five

Romans 16:17-18

Beware - Division

Quarreling groups in the church do not represent God's purpose. Some might be very sincere in their "common-sense" advice or desire to lead. Oswald Chambers states in <u>My Utmost for His Highest</u>: "It is easier to serve God without a vision, easier to work with God without a call, because then you are not bothered by what God requires; common-sense is your guide, veneered over with Christian sentiment."

As verse 18 says, "by smooth talk (common-sense) and flattery they (those who cause divisions and put obstacles in your way) deceive the minds of naive people."

If a brother approaches us about our usefulness or how valuable we would be serving here or there, or tries to encourage us on church/budget matters, we had best stop and beware! Is our good buddy's advice based on "common-sense" or "business sense"?

This "sense" does not put Jesus Christ as the guide as to where we should go or what we should do. Paul warns us to "keep away from them. For such people are not serving our Lord Christ, but their own appetites." (Romans 16:17-18)

Remember, it's GOD "sense" that will set us FREE! When God chooses to work - it works!

My Quiet Time Significant Journey Journal

1.   Ready yourself for a Fresh encounter with God. Pray and ask God to speak to you. (Psalm 37:7)

2.   Read the Scripture of the Day and prepare to hear a **Fresh Word** from God. (II Timothy 3:16-17)

3.   Respond with the *"**Mind of Christ**"* by writing down what God has said to you through the Scripture and the devotional thoughts. (Jeremiah 33:3)

4.   Reflect as you *"**Experience God**"* by listening to His Voice and writing down your prayers and thoughts. (John 16:23)

5.   Rely on Jesus to help you live out these truths. (Luke 11:28) Ask, ***"Lord, what do you want me to do today?"***   (God's to-do list.)

(Pray for strength as you put on the Full Armor of God.)

Week Sixteen - Day Six

Romans 16:19-20

Honesty! Be Wise!

As Paul talks to his faithful followers he assures them that he is proud of them and that he knows they are honest. But he says, to be smart, to be wise, and to make sure every "good" thing is the <u>real</u> thing.

Paul strikes a fine balance as he warns Christians not to ignore Satan. At the same time we are not to be paranoid about him. That he is real and dangerous goes without saying. But he is defeated! His days are numbered! The devil is like a roaring lion seeking whom he may devour, but remember he is on a short leash and the hand that holds the leash is the hand of God.

Rest assured, the God of peace, our Lord, will come down on Satan with both feet, stomping him into the dirt. (Romans 16:12) We must know where we stand and be careful how we live, but always with assurance and security in knowing that God has got our backs.

So stay alert! Be wise!

There is victory in Jesus!

My Quiet Time Significant Journey Journal

1. **Ready yourself** for a Fresh encounter with God. Pray and ask God to speak to you. (Psalm 37:7)

2. **Read** the Scripture of the Day and prepare to hear a **Fresh Word** from God. (II Timothy 3:16-17)

3. **Respond** with the **"Mind of Christ"** by writing down what God has said to you through the Scripture and the devotional thoughts. (Jeremiah 33:3)

4. **Reflect** as you **"Experience God"** by listening to His Voice and writing down your prayers and thoughts. (John 16:23)

5. **Rely** on Jesus to help you live out these truths. (Luke 11:28) Ask, **"Lord, what do you want me to do today?"** (God's to-do list.)

(Pray for strength as you put on the Full Armor of God.)

Week Sixteen - Day Seven

Romans 16:21-27

All Praise to Our God

Paul continues to send greetings to his fellow workers. His closing statements give a final explanation "of the mystery, which was kept secret since the world began." (Romans 16:25)

Can we believe this man Paul? As a servant, a devoted slave, set apart and called to belong to Jesus Christ who gives us hope, he says that <u>all believers</u> are saints loved by God with a calling from Christ. (Romans 1:7)

Paul directs our attention to God and makes it clear that God has the power to keep us in faith and obedience. God is the one who intervened. His was the wisdom that devised the glorious blending of grace, mercy and justice. It was His Son who died and it was this power that raised Him from the dead. It was from His right hand that the Spirit was dispensed and through Him that the redeemed believer lives the life that honors this Lord and crushes Satan.

The mystery that was kept secret for so long is now revealed and made known in an open book through the prophetic scriptures. Now all the nations of the world can know the truth, believe and obey!

"To the <u>only</u> wise God, through Jesus Christ—

to Him be the glory forever! Amen."

Here we Stand...Here we Live!

Amen and Amen!

My Quiet Time Significant Journey Journal

1. Ready yourself for a Fresh encounter with God. Pray and ask God to speak to you. (Psalm 37:7)

2. Read the Scripture of the Day and prepare to hear a **Fresh Word** from God. (II Timothy 3:16-17)

3. Respond with the *"Mind of Christ"* by writing down what God has said to you through the Scripture and the devotional thoughts. (Jeremiah 33:3)

4. Reflect as you *"Experience God"* by listening to His Voice and writing down your prayers and thoughts. (John 16:23)

5. Rely on Jesus to help you live out these truths. (Luke 11:28) Ask, *"Lord, what do you want me to do today?"* (God's to-do list.)

(Pray for strength as you put on the Full Armor of God)

About the Author:

Dr. Garry Baldwin has ministered and Pastored Churches across North Carolina and has led Mission Teams around the World for over 40 years. Since 2004, he has served here in Charlotte at Midwood Baptist Church in the Plaza Midwood/NoDa area. His love for discipleship inspired him to begin teaching at Charlotte Christian College and Theological Seminary to train and mentor Urban Pastors. A Graduate of The Citadel, Southeastern Baptist Theological Seminary, and Carolina Graduate School of Divinity, Dr. Baldwin seeks to challenge the Church to share the Gospel in their everyday life in a simple and clear way. Dr. Baldwin has been married to Cheryl since 1976 and has 3 grown children and 2 grandchildren.

Made in the USA
Coppell, TX
22 December 2019